Retail and Wholesa
Trade Services
in Canada

THE ECONOMICS
OF THE SERVICE SECTOR
IN CANADA

Series Editors:
Herbert G. Grubel
Michael A. Walker

Retail and Wholesale Trade Services in Canada

Keith Acheson and
Stephen Ferris

THE FRASER INSTITUTE

This study is part of a general programme of research into the services sector made possible by a contribution from the Department of Regional Industrial Expansion, Government of Canada.

Canadian Cataloguing in Publication Data

Acheson, Keith, 1940-

Retail and wholesale trade services in Canada

(The Economics of the service sector in

Canada, ISSN 0835-4227)

Includes bibliographical references.

ISBN 0-88975-122-6

1. Retail trade - Canada. 2. Wholesale

trade - Canada. I. Ferris, J. Stephen.

II. Fraser Institute (Vancouver, B.C.).

III. Title, IV. Series.

HF5429.6.C2A34 1986   381'.1'0971   C88-091398-3

61, 372

Printed in Singapore.

CONTENTS

CHAPTER 6
CO-OPERATIVES AND GOVERNMENT MARKETING / 123

CHAPTER 7
ORGANIZATIONAL UMBRELLAS: FRANCHISES
AND SHOPPING CENTRES / 139

CHAPTER 8
CONCLUSION / 159

Tables and Figures

Tables

Figures

PREFACE

This study is one of a number of specific industry reports undertaken for the Fraser Institute to analyse the significance of the "service" aspect of output in particular service industries. Our area is the trade or distribution sector (i.e., the wholesale and retail trade industries). The introductory chapters of the study present traditional measures of industry output and input. There are, however, unique spatial, public goods, informational and bundling issues that are qualitatively different from those affecting goods industries. In particular, the inability to observe economically the individual services provided and the difficulty of measuring the separate dimensions of the transactions arising in this sector create a number of problems for the public official or private participant interpreting these traditional figures.

Interestingly, the measurability and informational issues provide a common thread that link assessing factor performance and creating and keeping consumer confidence, a thread that helps explain the existence of particular trading institutions and contractual forms and their evolution through time. Through these institutions information is processed about the demands of individual consumers and the costs of meeting them.

Building and maintaining a fixed distribution system is an impressive physical accomplishment, but the distribution system is more than just a collection of physical entities. The distribution system embodies a competitive process with its own inner dynamic. Distributors both recognize and respond to the fact that consumers provide some of the inputs into shopping, that consumers are not well-informed of available values, and that potential customers are suspicious that promises of quality will not be delivered. Where creativity in "goods" sectors often takes an innovative physical form, the equivalent of the better mousetrap in the trade sector is originality in organizational form. This creativity permits the better co-ordination of the combined resources of the shopper and the shopkeeper.

Organizational innovation requires a different framework for analysis. A major portion of our analysis is designed to set out a theory of organizational behaviour as a response to the types of measurement problems described in the early chapters. The theory is illustrated by examining the contractual arrangements used in the private sector of the trade industry; the establishment of reputation, and the ability to exploit that investment through single ownership and the chain structure; the role of co-operatives and government retailing; and group solutions between multiple owners linked by private contracts, such as in franchising and shopping centres.

ACKNOWLEDGEMENTS

The industry detail in this report would not have been possible without the voluntary assistance of a number of members of this industry. We would like to single out a few for special mention. Mr. Gerry Snider of Statistics Canada, one of the authors of the definitive study, *Marketing in Canada,* provided initial encouragement and his division kept us constantly aware of the statistical detail; Mr. Alistar McKichan, President of the Retail Council of Canada, shared with us his association's experience with such issues as the Universal Product Codes and franchising; Mr. Don Collins of the Retail, Wholesale and Department Store Union ably represented the view of the labour movement towards such issues as franchising; and Mr. Jim Bennett of the Canadian Federation of Independent Businessmen shared with us the concerns of the small independent businessman. In addition we would like to thank Ms. Wendy Watkins of the Social Science Data Archives, Carleton University; Mr. Andrew Baldwin of Statistics Canada; Ms. Jane Billings and her staff at the Department of Regional and Industrial Expansion (DRIE); Ms. Rachel Acheson of the University of Virginia; and Ms. Karen Pianosi of the Municipality of Ottawa. Finally, we would like to thank Herb Grubel and Michael Walker for involving us in this project and for providing the overview that kept this work in perspective.

Our special thanks go to Hugh Acheson and Ina Ferris whose refusal to continually discuss retail and wholesaling issues and constant willingness to provide first-hand retailing experience provided the sanity and the motivation to finish this study.

ABOUT THE AUTHORS

Keith Acheson teaches economics at Carleton University. He earned his Ph.D. from the University of Toronto, and has taught at Queen's University and the University of Toronto.

His research interest is economic theory and its application to understanding the behaviour of organizations and markets. In 1977, he was a co-recipient of the annual Harry Johnson award for the best article in the *Canadian Journal of Economics.*

J. Stephen Ferris teaches economics at Carleton University. He received his B.Comm. and M.A. degrees from the University of Toronto and, after teaching at the University of Prince Edward Island, he returned to do his Ph.D. degree at the University of California, Los Angeles. Before joining Carleton, he taught at Simon Fraser and York Universities.

Professor Ferris' research interests lie in the areas of transaction costs and property rights. In these areas he has published articles in such journals as the *Canadian Journal of Economics, Economic Inquiry,* and the *Quarterly Journal of Economics.*

Chapter 1

THE TRADE SECTOR AND SHOPPING: OVERVIEW

THE TRADE SECTOR AND SHOPPING

If goods and services could be transferred without cost from producers to consumers, and if all the information relating to the quantities and qualities of goods and services were known, as were the particulars of where and when to distribute them, there would be no need for a trade sector. Manufacturers would interact directly with final consumers, and organizations such as stores and shopping centres would not exist. Warehouses would become museums and museums would display models of how life was in the "shopping" era.

Unfortunately, museum curators will have to focus their attention elsewhere for the foreseeable future. A surprisingly large share of our scarce resources is used to co-ordinate and transfer production to consumers. In 1986, for example, almost 14 percent of Gross Domestic Product was absorbed in the activities conducted by the trade sector.[1]

Comparing the Wholesale and Retail Sectors

The trade sector encompasses both the retail and wholesale sectors. The wholesale sector intermediates exchange among manufacturers and between manufacturers and retail stores, while the retail sector forms the final link in the distribution chain connecting producers with final consumers. As output moves up the distribution ladder, the size of the average transaction falls. This implies that buyers have less incentive to acquire information on product characteristics, and this information asymmetry produces important consequences for the organization of selling in the two markets. In the retail sector, sellers invest to develop brand names and institute such trade practices as liberal return and guaranteed low-price-matching policies to reduce consumers' fears of misrepresentation. Larger transaction sizes at lower distribution levels produce wholesale establishments that are usually larger than retail units and operate over broader geographic areas. This in turn implies that wholesaling will exhibit a greater degree of spatial concentration than will retailing.[2]

There are many similarities as well as differences between the retail and wholesale sectors. Both sectors are involved in the common functions of intermediation: storing goods, anticipating the demands of customer groups, searching out better products and better methods of delivering services, and bearing the risks of incorrectly reading the market.

The Shopping Activity

The demand for the services of the wholesale and retail trade sectors derives from what we will call the "activity of shopping." This activity is necessarily two-sided: inputs are provided by the trade sector and combined with time and other inputs provided by consumers to produce "shopping"— the transfer of goods and services. It follows that the productivity of shopping will increase whenever time or any other shopping input is economized upon. Most commonly, the increase in productivity occurs when innovation permits a reduction in those inputs used by the trade sector. What is not obvious, however, is that an *increase* in the resources used by the trade sector can also be consistent with an increase in productivity, *if* there is a more than commensurate fall in the inputs used by the buyer. The shifting importance of what is done by the trade sector and what is done by consumers in providing shopping services is an important and fascinating part of the evolution of the trading process. The various dimensions along which this boundary can change make the identification and measurement of industry output difficult and the interpretation of productivity problematic.

Commercial Inputs into Shopping: The Trade Margin

Because the trade sector intermediates exchange between manufacturers and consumers, its output is often measured as the margin by which the final selling price exceeds the sector's cost of acquiring the product (gross margin). With some items price exceeds the factory cost (plus freight) by a considerable amount, and markups of greater than 100 percent can arise. The existence of a margin does not necessarily imply the presence of market power in the intermediation process. Competition among potential traders constrains the price that trade intermediaries can charge and drives the value of the services provided by intermediaries into line with their costs. These costs will include a premium for the risk borne by intermediaries and the opportunity cost of acquiring capital.

That markups generally reflect the provision of value and not market power is suggested by the absence of significant entry barriers into the industry and by the substantial amount of real resources absorbed in distribution. In 1986, for example, labour employment in the trade sectors exceeded that in manufacturing and, in the decade preceding 1986, trade sector employment grew by 20 percent while manufacturing employment has remained roughly constant.[3]

Consumer Inputs into the Shopping Activity

While the retail price overstates the contribution of the trade sector to shopping, the cost of shopping exceeds the retail margin because of the inputs supplied by consumers and other commercial sources besides the retail store. One of the most important inputs provided by consumers is time. Shopping time includes the time taken to travel to and from the store, to find the product in the store, to obtain information about in-store varieties, and to queue for final payment. Before the shopper gets to the store, time is spent acquiring information on price and quality of comparable products, different store options, store opening hours, and transportation alternatives. Prior even to a decision to buy, a consumer interested in buying a squash racquet, for example, will discuss alternatives with friends, buy a consumer magazine that rates racquets, and read about the characteristics of a graphite racquet in a sports magazine, article, or advertisement. Not only is the consumer concerned with the performance characteristics of the racquet (what can it do and how reliably can it do it), but he or she is also concerned with the quality of ancillary information on how to maintain it. In addition, the consumer seeks information on durability and the characteristics of warranties and post-purchase service.

Another input that is usually provided by the shopper is transportation. Transportation services can be purchased by taking a bus or taxi. Alternatively, shoppers can drive and incur transportation costs through their payments for gasoline, maintenance, vehicle depreciation, and parking fees. Shoppers can reduce costs by sharing the driving, by incorporating the shopping activity into a trip to work, or by combining it with other social activities. This bundling of shopping with other activities makes it difficult, and in some cases impossible, to disentangle a separate cost of shopping. Transportation costs also interact with retailers' location decisions. A product may be sold through many small stores, decreasing the consumer's cost of travel between home and the nearest store. Alternatively, the product may be sold in larger stores (situated longer distances apart) that may offer different service dimensions (such as more convenient parking) that can more than compensate for the longer distance.

The expected costs of shopping to the consumer must also include the chance that a shopping trip will be unsuccessful. The store may be closed. The product may be out of stock or priced higher than expected. The store may not cash cheques, or take credit cards. The parking situation or line-ups may raise the expected waiting time to such an extent that the shopper decides to return when there is less congestion. All of these costs (like the transportation case above) are influenced by the inputs provided by the retailer. Longer hours require additional staff, larger stocks require greater storage, and easier access requires different spatial structures. These costs interact in turn with the inventory decisions, advertising strategy, and credit policies of retailers and wholesalers.

The value of the material inputs provided by the shopper is difficult to estimate. For shoppers who use their own cars for travel, depreciation on the capital value of the car must be estimated. While this calculation is difficult to make for transportation investments, these difficulties are minor when compared with those of assessing the value of the informational capital held by the consumer.

The information collected by a consumer is a capital asset that provides a flow of services for successive shopping trips. To see this, consider the dramatic increase in the cost of shopping that occurs when you move to a new location. In a new place, some of the most difficult answers are those to such commonplace questions as: Where is the freshest bread sold? Who has the best assortment of fruit? Which clothing stores stock my styles, in my price range? Are the supermarkets open on Tuesday nights? Why are they towing away my car? One response to the information problems of travellers is provided by the brand names of chains, department stores, and franchises that promise to consumers distinctive qualities that are uniform over many towns and cities. A stranger is more likely to shop or eat in brand name outlets than a native who has acquired the informational capital to shop or eat in the more interesting and idiosyncratic stores or restaurants.

Evaluating the Consumer's Inputs

While it is easy to think of information as a capital asset, it is more difficult to actually measure the value of the asset and the rate of its economic depreciation. In equilibrium, the value of an informational asset equals its cost of production at the margin. Since information is obtained through the expenditure of time, part of the problem is to identify (and evaluate) the time absorbed in this activity.

A measure for the value of time is also necessary to assess the value of the other time inputs into shopping. If the consumer could adjust the time input of all activities by small increments, then the time spent in all activities, including shopping, would be valued equally at the margin. If, in addition, work was valued only for the income generated, then more shopping time could be evaluated by the net income forgone. However, given the institutional impediments to allocating time marginally between work, leisure, and shopping (such as the discontinuity implied by a nine-to-five job), the value of time spent shopping may be considerably less (or more) than the payment for time spent working. Similarly, individuals frequently choose to work in jobs with lower salaries because these jobs more than compensate with on-the-job satisfaction. In this case the wage rate understates the value of time at the margin.

Casual empiricism also reveals that many individuals enjoy shopping as an activity, independent of whether a purchase is made or not. Taking this into account reduces the imputed cost of shopping.

INSTITUTIONAL RESPONSE

Attributes of Merchandising Services

Stores and wholesalers can increase their profits by offering customers goods and ancillary services that lower their total cost of shopping. The attributes of successful merchandising strategies reflect the constraints on coordinating buyers and sellers. First, trading services are typically bundled together with the product, being sold and priced as a single output. The tied nature of the final sale means that many consumer choices are discrete rather than continuous. Secondly, many trading services provided by retail and wholesale outlets are public goods (such as store hours and information). Thirdly, diverse products with distinctive mixes of salient shopping characteristics and customers with different wealth, information, and tastes encourage the creation of specialized institutions or new contractual arrangements. Finally, the importance of scale economies in distribution as well as in developing and exploiting brand reputations, of conglomeration economies in reducing search, and of scope economies in shopping, influences institutional response.

Vertical and Horizontal Integration and Partial Integration through Contract

The resulting variety and richness of organizational responses distinguish the trade sector and make its analysis interesting. Integration and divestment are constantly redefining the boundaries of the trade sector and its subsectors. Vertical and horizontal integration bring previously separately-owned entities under common ownership, changing the behavioural incentives and constraints facing their members. Placing separate activities under common ownership reduces the incentive for individuals in the individual parts to behave strategically with one another and can therefore remove barriers that prevent jointly beneficial actions being undertaken.

Vertical or horizontal integration represents only one "organizational" way of realigning incentives. Intermediate forms of integration can arise through contract. For example, a supply contract between a manufacturer and a wholesaler may have restrictions over the territory in which the product can be sold, or a manufacturer may sell directly to a dealer who is granted an exclusive right to market a product in return for promotional, display, and other commitments. Contractual arrangements placing limitations on behaviour are widespread in retailing and are particularly evident in franchise arrangements. The recent growth in franchising and other forms of market organization with vertical restraints represents dramatic changes in organization that have passed relatively unnoticed because they have not affected statistics such as concentration ratios or frequency of mergers, which are generally interpreted as signals of structural change.

While contractual limitations are viewed with suspicion by the competition authorities, economists are becoming increasingly aware that these contracts can increase economic efficiency by providing an appropriate framework of rewards.[4] This is likely to occur in situations where trading economies require lumpy transaction-specific investments by one party and where it is difficult to tell whether mutually agreed-upon obligations have actually been performed (so that contracts may be enforced economically). For example, it is frequently difficult for a supplier to verify and reward a retailer for providing the appropriate amount of product information to a buyer. By adding restrictions to contracts, individual incentives may be restructured in ways that result in a better mix of products, after-sale service, reliable information, and more efficiently located stores. Exclusive territories, for example, restrict spatial competition and thus permit the use of transportation costs to protect the rent generated by retailers who provide costly information services. Without some protection retailers who provide information are susceptible to free-riding from non-service-providing rivals, and in equilibrium, too little information will be supplied.

Competitive Experimentation

In the trade sector, efficiency is promoted through the continuous experimentation by individuals and groups among organization types that include corner stores, discount outlets, department stores, chains, franchises, shopping malls, and direct-mail outlets. Across these organizational forms, competition exists in the scope of products that are offered to customers, resulting in portfolios of store products that are constantly in flux. Drugstores expand into food and general merchandise lines at the same time as food stores add books and non-prescription drugs. Gasoline retailers drop repair services and add self-service food and entertainment. Canadian Tire successfully combines automotive, hardware, and household items while becoming the second-largest issuer of paper money in the country. Competition also arises across legal categories. The legal distinctions formalize packages of incentive, enforcement, and sharing provisions that permit single proprietorships and partnerships to contest for the consumer's dollar with small corporations, multinational giants, consumer and producer co-operatives, and government-owned stores.

These players compete in an environment determined by common law, competition policy, specific issue legislation (statutes concerning pyramid franchising and the revelation of terms in consumer financing contracts), and local and provincial laws that govern such shopping dimensions as opening hours, labour laws, and zoning regulations. The most recent legal changes affecting the trade sector concern the issues of comparable worth, the obligations of employers to part-time workers, the regulation of store hours, and local zoning and planning ordinances.[5]

OVERVIEW OF THE STUDY

Our study is concerned with a number of issues which are ultimately driven by informational or measurement problems. In chapter 2, we present a selection from the set of retail and wholesale output measures currently available to researchers as well as an analysis of their relation to economic activity, demographic factors, and financial conditions. (Our most interesting finding here was that at the aggregate level, population has not been a significant determinant of retail sales.) The contribution of the trade sector to Gross Domestic Product is then described relative to that of the manufacturing sector in Canada and relative to that of the trade sectors in other countries. Next we present a description of the major inputs used by the trade sectors; i.e., aggregate labour employment and its distribution relative to sales across Canada, as well as aggregate measures of capital. The chapter concludes with a description of the types of technical innovations that have impacted on the trade sector and discusses the role of government in relation to the innovation process.

In chapter 3, using the descriptive statistics of the preceding chapter, ratios of real sales and real value added per trade employee and per unit of capital are developed to evaluate sector performance. These measures are compared with measures of productivity in the trade sector derived from recent studies of productivity in the Canadian economy. A number of problems of applying traditional productivity approaches to the trade sector are also discussed. The intention is not to deter the calculation or use of such ratios but to provide a framework for their interpretation.

In chapter 4, we analyse in more detail an important measurement issue on the input rather than the output side of the market. Our objective is to go beyond the aggregate variables that can be used to account for earnings differences (outlined in the beginning of the chapter) to explore some of the more fundamental factors that could account for (a) a significant earnings differential between the retail sector and the rest of the economy and (b) a significant earnings differential in that sector between married men and other employees. The latter issue has particular policy relevance because of the recent growth in legislation seeking to remove gender earnings differentials and the important role played by part-time women in the retail sector. With the use of a much more detailed data base, we are able to shed more light on the likelihood that this differential can be attributed to discrimination.

Chapters 5, 6, and 7 form the analytical centre of our study. In chapter 5 we set out a theory of organizational behaviour, as a response to the types of measurement problems described in the earlier chapters, and illustrate the theory with respect to the contractual arrangements used in the private sector of the trade industry. The focus is on the establishment of reputation and the ability to exploit that investment through single ownership and the chain structure. Chapter 6 explores the comparative advantages and disadvantages of co-operatives in co-ordinating distribution. A non-private distribution system, the government liquor monopoly, is examined and assessed in the same chapter. Chapter 7 extends this analysis to group solutions between multiple owners through private contracts such as in franchising and shopping centres.

NOTES

1. Statistics Canada, *Gross Domestic Product at Factor Cost by Industry*, (61-213). See chapter 2 below for more detail.

2. William Coffey, "Locational Issues in Service Industries," talk at the Toronto meeting of the Service Sector Project (Forthcoming Institute for Research on Public Policy), 1988.

3. Statistics Canada, *Historical Labour Force Statistics*, CANSIM series D772006 and D773266.

4. Contractual constraints work to increase efficiency by restricting some forms of competition in order to enhance other areas of competition. By limiting competition, however, they may serve to enhance market power. The rapid growth of the economics literature in this area reflects the measurability problems of separating these diverging influences. See our discussion in chapters 5, 6, and 7.

5. For more on store shopping hours, see Stephen Ferris, "Time, Space and Shopping: The Regulation of Store Hours," Carleton Working Paper, November 1987.

Chapter 2

MEASURABLE OUTPUTS AND INPUTS

INTRODUCTION

The retail and wholesale trade industries perform the economic function of bringing the demands of final consumers together with the potential supplies of primary and secondary producers in Canada and abroad. Traditionally, this function has been called "distribution" at the wholesale level and "marketing" at the retail level. It consists of such activities as: displaying goods, informing consumers of product and service attributes, reducing the cost of search by shoppers and making it more convenient, identifying slow-moving or unprofitable product lines for manufacturers, arranging for the legal transfer of goods and services as well as credit and/or cash payment terms, and storing inventories and shifting them to more attractive locations while protecting them against theft and the deterioration of quality when in storage or on display. While the trade sector's output is intermediation, through the trade sector flow the goods and services produced by the private sector of the economy. The final sales of the trade sector meter the pulse of economic activity and are often used as a measure of its health.

While the primary purpose of our study is to emphasize the complexity of organizational forms used to co-ordinate the services performed by the trade sector, this chapter is devoted to setting out the aggregate dimensions of the trade sector and explaining how they interrelate with the economy. The chapter begins with a description of size of the trade sector as measured by final retail sales and investigates the role that macro aggregates have played in influencing the trade sector's growth. The analysis then turns to real value added as a measure of the contribution of these sectors to aggregate activity. This contribution is compared to that of manufacturing, and the position of trade in Canada is compared to that in Britain, West Germany, France, and the U.S. The second half of the chapter presents a description of the inputs used to intermediate trade and a comparison of the distribution of these inputs and outputs across the provinces.

CHARACTERISTICS OF RETAIL AND WHOLESALE SALES

Retail Sales

The total dollar value of the sales made by the retail sector is the market measure of the value (i.e., willingness to pay) placed by Canadians on the final goods and services sold by the retail sector. In 1986, this totalled $140 billion or almost 30 percent of the value of all final goods and services sold that year.[1] Over the period 1972 to 1986, nominal retail sales grew at a rate of 9.8 percent per annum, while GNP grew at the slightly faster rate of 10.7 percent. Adjusting for the rapid rates of inflation that occurred in that time period, the compounded annual rate of growth of real sales was 2.1 percent, compared with 2.5 percent for real GNP.[2] In per capita terms, real sales and real income have both grown by over 25 percent in this period. These are represented in figure 1.[3] As that figure illustrates, growth in per capita terms was not continuous but was interrupted by the dramatic decline in real values during the 1981–82 recession. The fall in real per capita values that signalled the arrival of that recession and the longer, more gradual period of recovery since has dominated the retail experience of the last decade.

Information on the level of retail sales in Canada is collected from surveys undertaken monthly by Statistics Canada (*Retail Trade, 63-005*). These surveys are conducted for stores selling products included in the 600 SIC (Standard Industrial Classification) categories. The data collected is grouped into 28 product categories and further aggregated into six major business store groups: food products, general merchandise, apparel and accessories, hardware and furnishings, automotive products, and "other" store products (consisting largely of pharmacies, book stores, jewellers, sporting goods stores, and stores selling alcoholic beverages).[4]

It is apparent, simply by listing the types of products involved, that the aggregate consists of the sales of products that differ in the seasonal pattern of their sales as well as in their longer time trend. This is illustrated in figure 2, where the time series of the quarterly sales of some of the larger subcomponents of retail store sales are presented in index number form for more convenient comparison. As can be seen from that figure, the sales made by department stores show considerable regularity in the pattern of their annual sales around a time trend that is only slightly upwards. Food store sales display a different annual sales cycle, one that is smoother and whose timing is different from that of department stores. In addition, these sales grew somewhat faster. Motor vehicle sales, at least over this time period, have given little evidence of seasonality. The increase in these sales over the whole period can be broken into two distinct parts: the rapid rate of growth between 1977 and 1979, and the small negative rate of growth

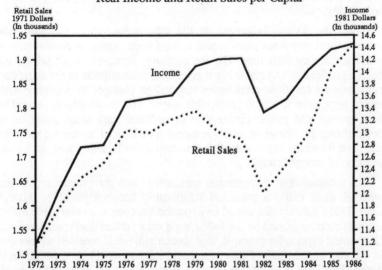

Figure 1
Real Income and Retail Sales per Capita

Sources: Retail Trade Historical Statistics (63-538); Retail Trade Monthly (63-005); CANSIM D1, D20000, D484000.

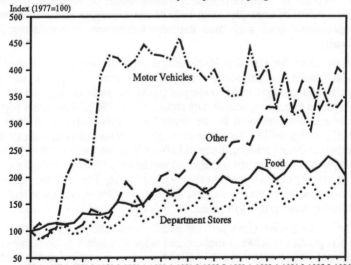

Figure 2
Retail Sales by Major Grouping

Sources: CANSIM (4911) D84659; (4914) D84818; (4917) D84915; (4920) D85020.

since then. "Other" retail products have exhibited systematic growth over this time period, with a pronounced but somewhat less regular pattern of seasonality.

Given the diverse behaviour of the subcomponents of the total, one might expect that retail sales would exhibit little aggregate consistency or predictability through time. On the contrary, however, retail sales have been a predictable and stable aggregate. Like consumption in the aggregate consumption function, retail sales respond to changes in economy-wide macro aggregates in highly predictable ways.[5] This predictability is used by both private and public planners to co-ordinate such retail activities as determining the size of advanced seasonal orderings, choosing the areas for chain or franchise expansion, and structuring the location, size, and composition of shopping malls.

The estimation of a regression equation is one procedure used to test whether there exists a statistical relationship between variables through time. That a relationship would be expected between sales and some macro aggregates is suggested by the following *a priori* theoretical considerations. One would expect, for example, that if each individual received an increase in income, at least part of that increase in income would be spent on retail goods. Similarly, a change in the rate of interest would be expected to affect an individual's choice of whether to save or spend. Increases in interest rates would lead individuals to increase their savings (consume tomorrow rather than today). Individual retail purchases would also be influenced by the probability of unemployment. Spending would be expected to rise as the probability of unemployment fell. At the aggregate level, changes in unemployment rates may also capture distribution effects across individuals.

To test these theoretical predictions and to determine the size of their effects in Canada, a regression of real retail sales (constant 1971 dollars) per capita was run against real income per capita, the interest rate, and the unemployment rate, using annual data from 1972 to 1986.[6] The actual regression results are presented in the appendix to this chapter and only the general findings will be discussed here. The regression results indicate that the group of three variables discussed above (income, interest rates, and unemployment rates) explain together approximately 94 percent of the variation in real per capita sales between 1972 and 1986. The relevant statistical tests on the whole equation suggest that there is very little chance that this relationship arose only by chance.

The separate predictions perform equally well. The positive relationship that was predicted between income and sales was found to be statistically significant, suggesting that a 10 percent increase in real per capita income would lead to more than a 13 percent increase in real retail sales per capita. Since the estimated income elasticity was greater than 1, retail sales fell into the category of luxury goods, at least for this time period. Similarly, increases in rates of interest and unemployment had their predicted negative effect on real sales per person. Although the estimated elasticities were small in absolute terms, the estimates were statistically significant, especially that between sales and interest rates.[7]

To test for the separate effect of population on retail sales, real retail sales were regressed against real income, population, the interest rate, and the unemployment rate. Once again the regression as a whole was highly significant (explaining 98 percent of the variation in real sales), and all of the individual variables had their predicted signs.[8] Only population did not perform as well as expected. While the test found that there was a small positive relationship between population and real retail expenditures, the relationship was not statistically significant. This suggests that in the aggregate (as opposed to any particular region) the number of consumers has been less important as a determinant of aggregate expenditure over this time period. One possible explanation is that the baby boom generation entering its high spending years has produced a demographic bulge in the age distribution that has distorted temporarily the traditional positive relationship between population and retail sales.[9]

With this background we can return to figure 1 and interpret the observed pattern of real retail expenditure per capita since 1972. The rise in real per capita expenditure that took place over this time period is explained primarily by rising levels of real per capita income. Figure 1 illustrates the remarkable conformity in the pattern of sales and income growth. The slower average rate of growth through the middle of the period and the more rapid rate of increase at the end are at least partially attributable to the effects of the rates of interest and unemployment. Rapidly rising interest rates, as early as 1979, resulted in a decline in real sales per capita leading into the 1981 recession. The increase in the unemployment rate generated by that recession, and the relatively slow rate at which it has declined, account for the slower rate of recovery (in Canada as opposed to the U.S.) of per capita retail sales.[10] Finally, the continued growth of retail sales (as compared to income) at the end of the time period was assisted by the fall in interest and unemployment rates through 1986.

Wholesale Sales

Measures of aggregate sales in the wholesale trade sector are less readily available. Prior to 1981, wholesale trade statistics were collected by separate surveys undertaken every other year by Statistics Canada for the two major subsectors of the industry (agents and brokers, and wholesale merchants).[11] Since 1981, consistent wholesale aggregates have been available, and these are presented in table 1.

Table 1

Total Retail and Wholesale Sales

(in millions)

	1981	1982	1983	1984
Wholesale Trade				
— Volume ($)	176,418	172,672	190,112	213,747
— Number of establishments	55,955	54,321	55,320	61,260
Retail Trade				
— Volume ($)	94,293	97,639	106,243	116,080

Sources: Statistics Canada, *Wholesale Trade Statistics*, 63-226; *Retail Trade*, 63-005.

Two points are of interest. First, the aggregate sales of the wholesale sector in Canada are larger than those of the retail sector. This initially surprising result is explained in part by the importance of trans-shipment and resale within the wholesale sector. Compared to the retail aggregate, there is a substantial amount of double counting in the industry sales total.[12] In addition, the wholesale sector sells a large part of its output to other commercial sectors of the economy besides the retail sector.[13] Finally, the importance of international trade for the Canadian economy means that some volume of trade goes through the wholesale sector prior to going abroad.

The second point worth noting is that in 1982 both the volume of trade and the number of establishments declined. This is the first indication of a different pattern of performance between the wholesale and retail sectors. That is, there appears to be a greater amount of cyclical fluctuation in the real variables of the wholesale sector than in the retail sector. As a rule, the wholesale sector exhibits behaviour that is closer to manufacturing than retailing.

The patterns of growth in quarterly sales of some of the important subsectors of the wholesale industry are shown in figure 3. Perhaps not surprisingly, only the wholesale food industry has exhibited a constant growth rate with the kind of cyclicality in sales that is typical of the retail sector. The lumber and building supplies industry and the machinery and equipment industry, on the other hand, have moved together over this period, without a discernible seasonal pattern but with a variability that has more closely followed the business cycle. Motor vehicle and accessory wholesalers, unlike their retailing counterparts, seem to have had a relatively uniform period of growth through the late seventies and early eighties.

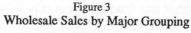

Figure 3
Wholesale Sales by Major Grouping

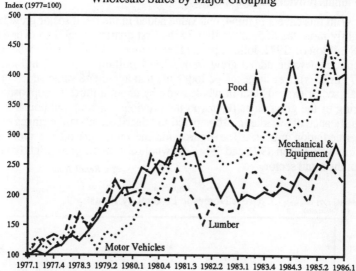

Index (1977=100)

Sources: CANSIM (4896) D84180; (4899) D84285; (4902) D84390; (4905) D84495.

REAL VALUE ADDED IN RETAIL AND WHOLESALE TRADE

The Value Added by the Domestic Trade Sector

The sales of the retail sector represent the value to consumers of the goods and services purchased from the retail sector. A substantial part of this, however, represents the value to consumers of acquiring goods that were produced in other sectors of the economy (such as manufacturing). The value to society of having a trade sector, then, is represented by the willingness of households to pay for the intermediation services of the trade sector—the many services of bringing producers of final products together with households.

While the distributive trades provide the setting and the facilities that bring these two sides together, it is clear that the activity of "shopping" also requires inputs from households as well as inputs provided by other commercial sectors of the economy. For most households, time is a substantial, self-provided input into the activity of acquiring goods and services, and the provision of transportation and information services by other service sectors frequently complements the services provided by the retail sector. This means that measures of value added in the trade sectors represent the willingness of consumers to pay only for the commercial part of the total provided by that sector, and that part may or may not move in parallel with the inputs provided by the shopper.[14]

With this caveat in mind, real value added in the retail sector grew from slightly more than $5,400 million in the first quarter of 1971 to over $10,-138 million (in 1971 dollars) by the first quarter of 1986.[15] In the wholesale sector, real value added grew from $3,914 million to $7,927 million (in 1971 dollars) over the same period. Note that aggregate value added in the retail sector exceeds that in wholesaling by about a third (the opposite ordering of the gross sales figures in the previous section) and points to the significance of "marketing" compared to "distribution" in the stages of the intermediation process. The figures for the entire period are plotted in figure 4. Between 1971 and 1986, the wholesale sector grew slightly faster than the retail sector.

Figure 4
Gross Domestic Product by Industry

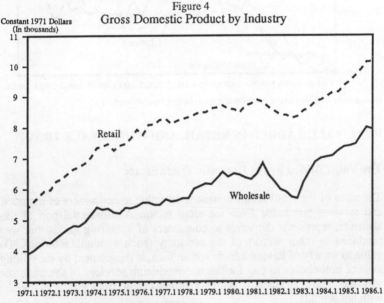

Source: CANSIM (1130) D144446, D144447, D144449.

Putting the wholesale and retail sectors together, the trade sector grew faster than manufacturing over this period and slightly faster than overall GDP. In terms of relative size, the trade sector accounted for 11.5 percent of GDP in 1971 and grew continuously to 13.5 percent of GDP by 1986. Real value added in the trade sector was only half the size of manufacturing at the beginning of the period, but this had grown to almost two-thirds by the end.

The relative growth of the wholesale and retail sectors is illustrated in figure 5. In that figure, real value added is expressed in the form of index numbers with the common base of 100 in 1971. Between 1971 and 1986, not only have both the retail and the wholesale sectors grown faster than GDP, but GDP in turn has grown faster than manufacturing. Cyclical variation is reflected most strongly in the manufacturing series. The 1974 oil crisis and the 1981–82 recession, for example, had a more dramatic impact on the manufacturing series than on the GDP series. What is also apparent is that the wholesale series exhibits the same time pattern of cyclicality as manufacturing, a pattern more striking when wholesaling is contrasted with retailing. The retail sector moves more closely in line with GDP. Compared with either manufacturing or wholesaling, the cyclical movements of the economy are merely suggested in retailing, rather than sharply defined.

Finally, the wholesale sector has grown relative to both retailing and manufacturing. The aggregate data, then, gives little support to the hypothesis that the wholesale sector is being squeezed by the forward integration of manufacturers and the backward integration of retailers. If anything, the relative growth in the value of the real resources used by the wholesale sector provides more support for the hypothesis that the wholesale sector is profiting from the disintegration of functions previously undertaken within the manufacturing sector.

While the retail sector aggregate exhibits relatively smooth movement through time, figure 6 illustrates that its subsectors do not. In this figure the growth of real value added in some of the important subcomponents was compared to the aggregate by dividing the subsector index of real value added by the index for the aggregate. A rise in that ratio above 1 means that that sector has grown relative to the sector total. On inspection, the smoothness of the aggregate illustrated earlier hides a considerable amount of movement within the aggregate. Some sectors, such as food stores and general merchandise stores, experienced a more or less continuous decline in real value added over this period, while other sectors such as drugstores grew dramatically. Similarly, changes in real value added in some sectors (food and drugs) seem countercyclical or independent of the business cycle, while in others (department and general merchandise stores) changes in real value added move with the retail aggregate over the cycle. Finally, some industries (e.g., motor vehicle dealers) have experienced movements in real value added that more than match the cyclical movement of the aggregate.[16]

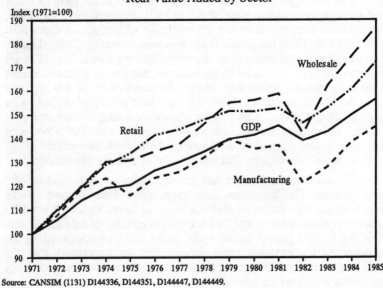

Figure 5
Real Value Added by Sector

Index (1971=100)

Wholesale
Retail
GDP
Manufacturing

1971 1972 1973 1974 1975 1976 1977 1978 1979 1980 1981 1982 1983 1984 1985

Source: CANSIM (1131) D144336, D144351, D144447, D144449.

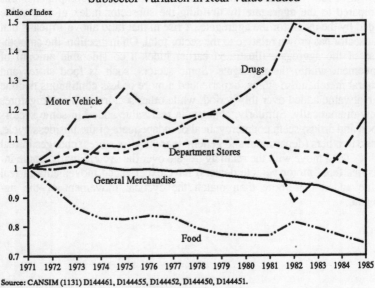

Figure 6
Subsector Variation in Real Value Added

Ratio of Index

Drugs
Motor Vehicle
Department Stores
General Merchandise
Food

1971 1972 1973 1974 1975 1976 1977 1978 1979 1980 1981 1982 1983 1984 1985

Source: CANSIM (1131) D144461, D144455, D144452, D144450, D144451.

Table 2

**The Percentage Contribution to GDP of Manufacturing and Trade
in the United Kingdom, the United States, Germany and Canada, 1980**

	Manufacturing	Trade
United Kingdom	21.4	12.5
United States	22.6	17.0
Germany	36.4	9.4
Canada	21.9	12.8

Sources: Smith and Hitchens, 1985, p. 5; Statistics Canada, 61-213.

Cross-Country Comparison of Real Value Added

The contrast in the size of the distribution sectors in different countries is illustrated in table 2. That table records the contribution to GDP in 1980 of the distribution and manufacturing sectors in the United Kingdom, the United States, Germany, and Canada.[17] The distribution categories across the first three countries were made consistent by adding the value added by car dealers, filling stations, and eating and drinking places to the distribution sector of the U.K. This made the U.K. definition comparable to that used in the U.S. and Germany.

A first look at the table suggests that Canada is closer to the U.K. than to the U.S. in terms of the contribution of its manufacturing and trade sectors to GDP. However, the omission of restaurants and other eating and drinking establishments from retailing in Canada produces a downward bias in the Canadian trade percentage.[18] Given that these industries account for approximately 3 percent of GDP in Canada, the Canadian number for trade approaches more closely the American number.[19]

These numbers are consistent with one's intuition that the Canadian economy resembles more closely the American economy in terms of its wholesale distribution network and retail marketing system. The greater distances of North America, combined with lower population densities and greater shopping mobility, provide major reasons why the trade sectors absorb a larger proportion of real resources in the North American economies.

LABOUR INPUTS

In figure 5, the growth in the size of the trade sector between 1971 and 1986 is illustrated in terms of value added. Figure 7 shows the same pattern in terms of employment.[20] In absolute terms, manufacturing employment grew only slightly over this 15-year period, while employment in the trade sectors has steadily risen.[21] By 1984, employment in the trade sector sur-

Figure 7
Total Employment by Sector

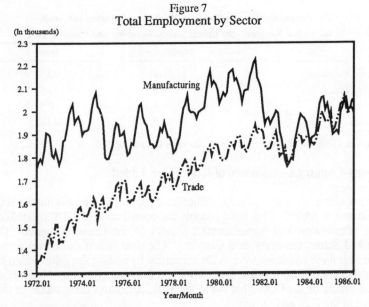

Source: CANSIM (2074) D772003, D772006.

passed that in manufacturing for the first time, and the gap between the two is increasing. Relative to total nonagricultural employment, however, employment in the trade sector has increased only slightly (rising from 17.5 percent to 18.5 percent of the total). On the other hand, manufacturing's share of nonagricultural employment fell from 23 percent in 1971 to 18 percent by 1986.

Although the trend in the fraction of employment accounted for by manufacturing has been downward, the fall in that ratio has not been continuous. Rather, the ratio has fallen in two periods: first, a large and continuous drop in the ratio following the 1974 oil crisis through 1977; and second, a shorter but more dramatic fall in late 1981 and 1982. The cyclical movement of the economy, then, is strongly reflected in the relative movement of labour employment in manufacturing. In addition, manufacturing exhibits considerable seasonality. Compared to this, employment in the trade sector presents relatively little evidence of cyclicality.[22] As can be seen from figure 7, there is little evidence of the oil shock in the trade employment series, and the 1981 recession is barely reflected in the data. Relative to the seasonal pattern of trade employment (rising in two peaks through Christmas and falling thereafter) and the relatively constant trend of growth over the whole period, the cyclical movement in trade employment is barely noticeable.

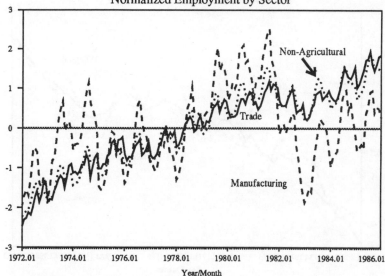

Figure 8
Normalized Employment by Sector

Source: CANSIM (2074) D772003, D772006, D769833.

In figure 8, the two employment series are normalized so that the pattern of seasonality, cyclicality, and time trend in the different series becomes apparent. Inspection of that figure indicates that the trade sector has been more successful than the manufacturing sector in absorbing the real cyclical shocks that have affected the economy and, somewhat more surprising, more successful in smoothing the seasonality of employment. The manufacturing series generates roughly twice the annual variation of the trade series. Relative to the rest of the nonagricultural sectors, employment in the trade sector has somewhat less variability over the year and over the cycle.

The pattern of annual and cyclical variation in employment can now be compared to that of real output with the use of figure 8 in conjunction with figure 9. In figure 9, the time series of real value added in the wholesale and retail trade sectors are normalized for comparison with manufacturing. Because the data is on a quarterly basis there is less scope for demonstrating the seasonality of the real value added series (in comparison with employment in figure 8); however, the quarterly data permits the cyclicality of the data to stand out more clearly. This figure confirms our earlier observation that the trade sector has considerably less cyclicality than manufacturing. Variability in the wholesale sector lies between the two other series, moving with the manufacturing sector through the cycle but with less varia-

Figure 9
Normalized Real Value Added

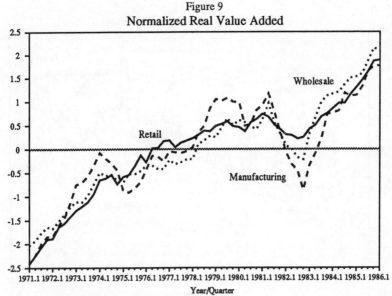

Year/Quarter

Source: CANSIM (1130) D144449, D144447, D144351.

tion over the cycle. Finally, the same order is preserved on an annual basis. In general, the retail series is the smoothest, followed by the wholesale and the manufacturing series.

We conclude our discussion of aggregate labour use by contrasting the distribution of wholesale and retail trade employment across the Canadian provinces with the provincial distributions of total labour force and retail sales. These are presented in table 3 for the census years 1971 and 1981.[23] The distinguishing feature of this table is the remarkable degree of uniformity in the provincial distributions across all variables.

CAPITAL INPUTS

Physical Capital

Growth in real capital stock has been an important factor in the real growth of the trade sector.[24] The real (net) capital stock of the trade sector has grown more or less constantly from $7,187.3 million in 1971 to over $10,685.0 million in 1986 (in 1971 prices). This corresponds to a real growth rate of 2.7 percent per year over the 15-year period. Throughout this period, however, the rate of increase in the capital stock has slowly fallen,

Table 3
Provincial Distribution of Sales and Employment

Province	Percentage of:	1971	1972	1981
NFLD	Total Canadian Retail Sales		1.9	1.8
	Total Canadian Labour Force	1.7		1.9
	Total Retail Employment	1.8		1.9
	Total Wholesale Employment	1.9		1.8
P.E.I.	Total Sales		.5	.4
	Labour Force	.5		.47
	Total Retail Employment	.45		.44
	Total Wholesale Employment	.5		.34
N.S.	Total Sales		3.2	3.1
	Labour Force	3.3		3.1
	Total Retail Employment	3.5		3.4
	Total Wholesale Employment	3.4		3.2
N.B.	Total Sales		2.6	2.5
	Labour Force	2.6		2.5
	Total Retail Employment	2.8		2.6
	Total Wholesale Employment	2.4		2.3
QUE	Total Sales		25.3	24.9
	Labour Force	25.1		25.3
	Total Retail Employment	23.4		24.6
	Total Wholesale Employment	22.6		23.9
ONT	Total Sales		38.3	35.3
	Labour Force	38.9		37.0
	Total Retail Employment	39.4		36.8
	Total Wholesale Employment	38.7		38.2
MAN	Total Sales		4.3	3.8
	Labour Force	4.8		4.2
	Total Retail Employment	4.9		4.2
	Total Wholesale Employment	4.8		4.7
SASK	Total Sales		4.0	4.0
	Labour Force	4.3		3.8
	Total Retail Employment	4.1		3.8
	Total Wholesale Employment	4.0		3.9
ALB	Total Sales		8.0	11.2
	Labour Force	8.0		10.0
	Total Retail Employment	8.0		10.0
	Total Wholesale Employment	8.6		10.9
B.C.	Total Sales		11.7	12.6
	Labour Force	10.5		12.0
	Total Retail Employment	11.3		12.0
	Total Wholesale Employment	11.6		12.0
Y & NWT	Total Sales		0.2	0.3
	Labour Force	0.2		0.2
	Total Retail Employment	0.2		0.2
	Total Wholesale Employment	0.1		0.1

Sources: Statistics Canada, *1971 Census*, 94-740, vol. III, table 2; *1981 Census*, 93-961, . . . 973, table 16; *Retail Trade Historical Statistics*, 1972-79, 63-538; *Retail Trade* (Monthly) 63-005, March 1982.

primarily because gross investment has stabilized.[25] As figure 10 illustrates, although aggregate real investment had increased from slightly over $500 million per year (in 1971 prices) to $800 million per year by 1986, the major part of that increase came in the first four years. Since 1974, investment has remained relatively constant.

Figure 10
Real Investment in Trade

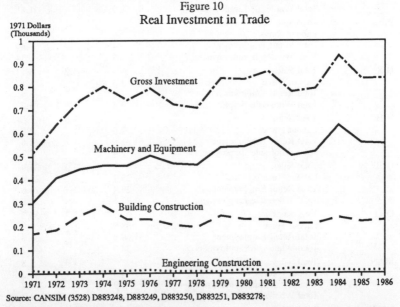

Source: CANSIM (3528) D883248, D883249, D883250, D883251, D883278;

Statistics Canada, Fixed Capital Flows and Stocks (13-211).

While total investment activity has not changed in recent years, there has been a gradual change in the composition of investment expenditures. Investments in machinery and equipment have grown both relative to investment in buildings and in absolute terms.[26] Figure 10 also reveals an interesting shift in the source of the fluctuations of aggregate investment. The downturn in aggregate investment that followed the 1974 oil shock, for example, arises primarily because of the rapid decrease in new investment in buildings. Investment in machinery and equipment was also affected but through a fall in the rate of increase rather than in level. The further fall in investment activity between 1976 and 1978 is reflected in both investment series, as is the following rise in investment activity coming out of that downturn. The closer one moves to the present, the more the variations in machinery and equipment begin to dominate movements in the series. The rapid rise in aggregate investment coming out of the 1981–82 recession is reflected almost entirely in the dramatic increase in machinery and equipment, and its fall-off later in the cycle is sufficient to produce a downturn in the aggregate.

Technical Change

The change in the composition of investment expenditure in the trade sector becomes less surprising when the rapid rate of technical change is taken into account. A considerable amount of the investment in machinery and equipment then corresponds to the purchase of technological change as embodied in the new types of machinery and equipment. New technology, particularly electronic technology, has had important effects on the distribution system. Computer technology, for example, has been useful in lowering distribution costs by permitting the integration of the sales, inventory, accounting, and ordering functions of retail and wholesale businesses. In grocery stores, for example, the scanning equipment that reads the Universal Product Code can also be combined with electronic registers with computer memories. In this way the reading and pricing economies of the checkout counter can be extended to automated inventory holding policies, optimal repurchasing plans, and the control and accountability functions of the firm's accounting procedures.[27]

What is not clear at this stage is how the information revolution that has accompanied the innovations in computer technology will impact on the organization of the retail and wholesale trade. For example, in the early stages, improvements in computer technology were used primarily to lower the cost of maintaining individual credit records, inventory holdings, and personal files, and undertaking large replicative accounting functions.[28] Such computer efficiencies accrued mostly to the larger firms and assisted in reducing some of the co-ordination costs that previously had restrained the growth in the size of the firm.[29] More recently, however, innovations in software technology have extended to the small firm the same types of co-ordination features that were previously affordable only by the largest companies.[30] Even the smallest retail store now has access at low cost to credit facilities that previously could be undertaken only by the largest department stores, and many small retailers currently use the billing, inventory, and accounting features of low-cost computer software packages. Recent innovations, such as the use of sales and inventory information to target the "direct profitability" of individual product lines, will continue to have profound effects on the nature and scope of competition within the industry. At present, there seems to be little reason to doubt the continuation of the current trend to assist the small retailer relative to its larger rival.

The illustration of computer-related innovations with reference to the grocery industry has not been arbitrary. Rather, the widespread adoption of information processing technology has been possible because of the existence of the Universal Product Code for grocery products. A parallel system of product coding for general merchandise, the Universal Product Code, has been developed and came into effect in January 1988.

The encouragement and active co-ordination of industry attempts to achieve greater standardization are important ways in which government can assist in enhancing industry performance. In more technical terms, the adoption of uniform industry standards poses problems of choice for the industry that are "total" rather than "marginal" in nature and thus are likely to generate larger externalities than will other market choices. In these cases, government co-ordination can often supplement the efficiency of the market by lowering the costs of achieving industry-wide agreement and enforcing against the opportunistic incentives that arise when joint action is desirable.[31] For example, in addition to playing a supportive role in the adoption of the Universal Product Code for general merchandise, DRIE can play a more active role in current efforts to develop greater standardization in shipment packaging through the development of a Universal Distribution Code. Greater standardization will permit the distribution sectors to exploit more fully the economies of modularization and automation in their storage and warehousing activities.

Looking to the immediate future, standardization issues are increasingly important in the rapid development of new payments systems and technologies. The development of the debit card, whereby bank deposits can be accessed directly by retailers (rather than indirectly through bank credit cards), appears imminent, although the debit card seems to be, at present, more popular with retailers than with final consumers. One suggested benefit of the debit (as opposed to credit) payment system is that the current system discriminates against smaller retail establishments by assessing proportionately higher fees to business firms experiencing smaller sales (and hence credit) volumes. The new debit card, it is argued, can be priced to reflect the costs of assessing the creditworthiness of customers, a cost that should be independent of the size of the retail establishment. If the technology of the debit card does permit a lowering of the costs of the final payments system, it should be possible for the industry to structure a fee schedule that would spread the net benefits so as to ensure the enthusiastic acceptance of the new technology. At present there is a considerable amount of world-wide experimentation in point-of-sale payments systems. Keeping Canadian retailers aware of developments around the world and reducing the costs of co-ordinating an overall system are appropriate activities of government. In playing a catalytic role in new technology, the government will be under pressure from different segments of the industry to accelerate or decelerate changes in the system and to alter the nature of the system for their benefit. The task of the government is to encourage the development of a system that does not impose arbitrary burdens on particular sectors and that is flexible and open to entry and future innovation.

Computer technology has permitted increasing centralization in information collection, while encouraging the decentralization of decision making. Many of the older distribution tasks, such as keeping track of inventories and maintaining a proper reordering schedule, are increasingly being delegated to software, freeing time for the marketing functions of the distribution system. The improved ability to gather and analyse information has made new marketing initiatives possible. In Canada, the current retail trend is towards stores targeting a particular type of customer (e.g., ethnic group, age category, sex, or lifestyle) and offering to those consumers a broader range of commodities than has traditionally been the case.

Finally, the retail and wholesale sectors, like the rest of the economy, have been strongly influenced by innovations in communication technology. The increased ability to target particular customer types has combined with innovations in publishing technology to bring a rebirth of the direct-mail business. Similarly, the dramatic extension in the number of channels offered by cable television creates opportunities for retailing that are only beginning to be realized.[32] The ability to merge the viewing advantages of television with the interactive capability of the computer permits electronic-assisted shopping from the home. This technology is at least a partial substitute for moving stores closer to the customer, and may assist in reducing the disadvantage that manufacturers and consumers have felt in the regions of the country that are distanced from large population centres.

Innovations Not Embodied in Capital

Technical improvements, from better fork-lift trucks in the warehouse to code readers at the supermarket checkout stand, are embedded in the capital equipment purchased by the trade sector. Organizational innovations also improve the co-ordination of resources in the trade industry, but their contribution is not as easily measured. Most often, organizational changes are made to overcome information asymmetries or other impediments to the effective co-ordination of trade. Advertising with new media, developing brand names, establishing franchising arrangements, and developing retail chains all address the issue of increasing economically the predictability of retail opportunities.

Shopping centres represent another type of organizational innovation. Through their ability to exclude, private owners use membership conditions to control collectively harmful, purely redistributive forms of competition and foster complementarities that increase individual returns through group activities. The use of differential site rents permits a shopping centre to take into account externalities that are generated by some retail outlets.[33] On the other hand, the shopping centre avoids the shirking problems associated with a single owner (such as a department store organization) and uses competition across stores to maintain the vibrancy of the organization.

Organizational innovations vary from those that are evident to a shopper only through lower prices or wider ranges of choice to those that change dramatically the pattern of life in rural and urban communities. The shopping centre, for example, has become a new form of urban park, with entertainment and other leisure activities sharing the stage with retailing. In many cities the mall is the focus of teenage life and family outings, while in a few the mall has grown to tourist proportions.[34]

Finally, technical improvements in those industries that supply inputs into the shopping activity can also influence the types and quantities of inputs demanded by the trade sector. For example, refrigerated trucks and boxcars allowed the distribution of perishable products over a wider domain and improved the delivered quality. This in turn permitted larger-scale farming operations and lower product prices. Advances in moving people, such as urban rapid transportation systems and automated traffic control, made movement and hence shopping cheaper. Both of these innovations affect store locations, investments in parking, merchandise mix in individual stores, and the average size of stores.

In this chapter we have concentrated on the measurable inputs and outputs of the trade sector. In the next, we turn to their use in measures of sector performance. At this point it is worth emphasizing that organizational innovation is perhaps the most distinctive feature of the trade sector and the primary way in which productivity gains are realized in this sector rather than being derivative of developments elsewhere. The role of organizations and their interaction with the "unmeasurable" outputs of the trade sector is the focus of chapters 5, 6, and 7.

NOTES

1. Preliminary estimate, Statistics Canada, *Retail Trade*, March, 1987, catalogue 63-005, table 28. p. 57. Retail sales were 29 percent of a Gross National Product of $488,408.0 million in 1986.

2. Compounded rates of growth were calculated by regressing the logarithm of the variable against time. The regression equations for real sales in constant 1971 dollars and real income in 1981 dollars are presented below as:

$$\log \text{(real retail sales)} = -31.45 + 0.0212 \text{ time,} \quad R^2 \text{adj.} = .810$$
$$(5.84) \ (7.81)$$
$$\log \text{(real income)} = -36.35 + 0.025 \text{ time,} \quad R^2 \text{adj.} = .860$$
$$(6.91) \ (9.32)$$

   Note: t-statistics in brackets.

3. See the appendix of this chapter for a more detailed description of data sources used and/or special calculations that were made for each figure.

4. In Canada, unlike the United States, restaurant and other eating and drinking establishments are not included in the retail sector.

5. The remainder of this section is based on the regression findings reported in the appendix of this chapter. They were calculated with TSP 5.1.

6. Note that the regression discussed in the text and presented in the appendix is in logarithms. This allows us to interpret the coefficients of the independent variables as elasticities. For an example of a provincial application of this approach, see *Employment and New Technology in the Retail Trade Industry*, Appendix 17 of the Ontario Task Force on Employment and New Technology, July 1985.

7. The estimated elasticities: 1.34 for real per capita income, -0.11 for the interest rate, and -0.03 for the unemployment rate.

8. Once again the regression was run in logarithmic form. The estimated elasticities for real income, population, interest rates, and the unemployment rate were, respectively, 1.24, 0.05, -0.11 and -0.07.

9. If the traditional relationship between population and sales has been distorted by the demographics of the baby boom, there is likely to be a corresponding offset in sales as this generation ages. To some extent

the market is responding to this challenge with a growth in marketing directed at the older age groups.

10. U.S. retail sales per capita bottomed in 1980, whereas the bottom was reached in Canada in 1982.

11. The distinction is that between an intermediary and an agent. That is, the wholesale merchant acquires ownership of the product passing through the distribution network and gains or loses depending on the difference between the buying and selling price. Agents and brokers do not acquire ownership and are paid a fee for the services performed. The two forms are, of course, substitutes, so that the choice of the institutional form should be explainable in terms of the same transaction cost theory described in chapters 5 through 7.

12. See Real Value Added in Retail and Wholesale Trade, below.

13. Note, for example, the sales that will arise to non-retail commercial sectors in the industries represented in figure 3.

14. Changes in the value added of the trading sector may arise merely because of a redistribution of activities from the trade sector to the other agents in the shopping process. Thus these changes will sometimes be misleading as a measure of the size, and often the direction, of the change in value added in "shopping." The history of the evolution of the wholesale and retail sectors through time reflects the evolution of the costs of providing shopping services indirectly through middlemen rather than between manufacturers and consumers directly. These measurement issues are the focus of chapter 3 of this study.

15. Real value added as discussed in this section of the text is measured as real (1971) Gross Domestic Product at factor cost, quarterly data on an annual basis. See the appendix for details.

16. When this ratio was formed for the subsectors of the wholesale sector, the ratio was found to stay constant over the whole period. The data gives no evidence of a change in the distribution of activities among the organizational alternatives.

17. The first three rows in this table are taken from A.D. Smith and D.M.W.N. Hitchens, *Productivity in the Distributive Trades: A Comparison of Britain, America and Germany*, Cambridge: Cambridge University Press, 1985, table I.I, p. 5.

18. In terms of the number of establishments or the volume of aggregate sales, eating and drinking establishments are about one-quarter of the size of the retail aggregate.

19. See, for example, D.J. Duncan and S.C. Hollander, *Modern Retailing Management: Basic Concepts and Practices,* 9th Edition, Homewood, Illinois: Richard D. Irwin, 1977, p. 15.

20. Note that employment in this figure refers to the number of employees and not the hours of work. Because of the relative growth of part-time employment in the trade sectors, the retail trade industries in particular, labour employment figures will overstate the relative growth of the trade sector relative to manufacturing.

21. Total trade employment grew at a compounded annual rate of 2.5 percent from 1,327,000 in January 1971 to 2,125,000 in December 1986. Manufacturing employment grew from 1,688,000 to 1,978,000 and total nonagricultural employment from 7,194,000 to 11,114,000 over the same period.

22. For more on seasonality in employment and the work of Statistic Canada on seasonality through its X11-Arima model see Statistics Canada, *Seasonal Variations in the Canadian Economy* (16-501). Our thanks to Andrew Baldwin for discussions on this topic.

23. To keep the sales data consistent throughout this chapter, aggregate sales for 1972 were used instead of 1971.

24. It is worth mentioning at this point that neither foreign ownership nor concentration of ownership are major policy issues in the trade sector, although in relative terms there is more concern at the wholesale rather than the retail level, and in particular geographic regions. See Statistics Canada, *Concentration and Foreign Control in Retail and Wholesale Trade in Canada,* 1979, Ottawa (63 - 539). See chapter 5 for more recent information.

25. It is important to note that inventories form a large part of distribution assets. For example, for the larger machinery and equipment and motor vehicle wholesalers, inventories are over 40 percent of total assets. Large wholesale food distributors hold between 30 and 35 percent of their assets in inventories. Of the large wholesale industries that are followed by Statistics Canada, only in lumber and building supplies has there been a dramatic fall in this ratio since 1977 (from 30 percent in early 1977 to 16 percent in early 1986). Source: CANSIM, Statistics Canada, Matrix Nos. 4895 for Food Distributors, 4898 for Motor

Vehicles, 4901 for Machinery and Equipment, and 4904 for Lumber and Building Supplies.

26. Note that in the retail sector there is increasing use of the policy of leasing rather than owning locations. This has meant that for a company like Canada Safeway, about 35 percent of total capital consists of merchandise inventories.

27. As an example of the pace of innovation through equipment, Canada Safeway had installed scanning systems in three of its stores in 1979, along with automated systems to regulate energy use. In 1981 an integrated computer system was adopted, so that by 1982 the scanners were interconnected with the computer network to control inventories and facilitate reordering (Safeway annual reports).

28. In recent hearings before the House of Commons Finance Committee it was pointed out that large retailers have used their credit card facilities both to induce customer loyalty and to generate superior information on their customers' demands. The scale economies involved are such that they are feasible for only the largest organizations (news summary of the hearings in *Globe and Mail,* Wednesday December 16, 1987, p. B6).

29. The rapid acceptance of the grocery superstore, where economies of scale have not come at the expense of specialty selection, is one dramatic example of this technology at work.

30. Perhaps nowhere is this more apparent than in desktop publishing, where virtually anyone with a personal computer and access to a laser printer can set up shop as a publisher.

31. Because the costs of adopting a new standard are lower for the individual who waits until the success of the new standard is guaranteed, there is always an inertia problem in switching to a new or common standard. Canada's experience with metric conversion is perhaps our most memorable recent example.

32. At the 1987 annual meeting of Canadian Home Shopping Network Ltd., the chairman, Mr. Golberg, announced plans to expand offerings on cable television into financial and travel services, and to spin off a direct-mail operation. At present CHSN is available to 5.02 million of the 6 million Canadian cable television subscribers.

33. A shoe repair outlet, for example, may not itself earn enough to cover the cost of its space in a shopping centre, but its presence may draw a sufficient number of customers to other stores to warrant its inclusion.

In a street environment, the side payments from other stores may be too costly to arrange (because any single store has an incentive to free-ride on the payments of others). In a centralized shopping centre, however, the owner can attract the shoe repair store through a lower rental rate and recover the lost revenue by renting the remaining space at higher average rates. Rules that require all centre stores to open and close at the same time, share in common expenses (such as parking and/or advertising), and conform to a common design are examples of these internalizing activities.

34. As an extreme example of what seems to be a particularly Canadian specialty, the West Edmonton Mall is now a major tourist attraction.

APPENDIX

Calculations used for the figures and regressions reported in the text:

1. In figure 1, to derive a comparable figure for real sales in 1986, the change in the 1981 implicit price deflator was used to calculate a 1986 figure for the implicit price deflator based on 1971 prices. The value used to deflate nominal retail sales in 1986 was 283.4. The real income measure used was Gross National Product per capita; it was calculated by dividing GNP by population and the consumer price index.

2. Regressions for real retail sales:

    The annual regression equation for real (1971) per capita retail sales between 1972 and 1986 is:

Dependent variable: Log (real retail sales per capita)	Coefficient	t-statistic
Independent variables:		
Constant	4.98	5.07
Log[real (1981) GNP per capita]	1.34*	12.38
Log(three-month treasury bill rate)	-0.11*	6.30
Log(unemployment rate)	-0.03**	1.78

Regression statistics: Adjusted R^2 = .942

Durbin-Watson = 2.01

F-statistic = 76.96

* (**) significantly different from zero at 5 percent (10 percent)

The annual regression equation for real (1971) retail sales over the same 1972–86 time period:

Dependent variable: Log (real retail sales)	Coefficient	t-statistic
Independent variables:		
Constant	-5.33	2.25
Log[real (1981) GNP]	1.24*	9.26
Log(population)	0.05	0.14
Log(three-month treasury bill rate)	-0.11*	6.39
Log(unemployment Rate)	-0.07**	1.92

Regression statistics: Adjusted R^2 = .981

Durbin-Watson = 2.15

F-statistic = 179.1

* (**) significantly different from zero at 5 percent (10 percent)

Additional data sources not reported with those for figure 1: *Bank of Canada Review*, series A1 for the three-month treasury bill rate on an annual basis and CANSIM, Statistics Canada, D767289, for annual unemployment rates.

3. In figure 5, seasonally unadjusted, monthly indexes are in constant (1971) prices; 1970 SIC, converted to annual figures through TSPs annual average conversion programme.

4. In figure 6, monthly indexes converted to annual basis.

5. In figure 8, the normalized values were calculated by subtracting the mean and dividing by the standard deviation so that the rescaled series can be compared in terms of their variation.

6. In figure 9, the normalized (quarterly) real value added series is derived as described above.

Chapter 3

MEASURING PRODUCTIVITY

INTRODUCTION

In the previous chapter we reported and discussed the aggregate measures of outputs and inputs that are traditionally used in the calculation of industry productivity. This chapter begins with an exploration of the difficulties in meaningfully interpreting the productivity measures derived from available data. The first difficulty derives from the importance of the inputs provided by the customer in the shopping activity. No satisfactory measures of these inputs and their change over time exist. This gap in our knowledge may also create problems in interpreting productivity measures based on data that summarize only what the commercial trade sector does.

In the next section, attention is focused on other issues in interpreting productivity ratios calculated from the various output and input measures, and techniques for combining them. In any industry there are problems when aggregating heterogeneous components of outputs or inputs into a total. However, the importance of spatial competition for distribution and the many dimensions of merchandising (providing information, reducing search costs, credit, implicit guarantees, atmosphere, and so on) make the measurement of output particularly difficult. Having presented these caveats, we then discuss a number of different productivity measures.

THE SHOPPING ACTIVITY

In the activity of shopping, the many inputs of shoppers (time, informational capital, and physical capital) are combined with buildings, machines, and labour provided by the commercial trade sector. To derive changes in the labour productivity of shopping, a series of shopping outputs and series on the total labour provided by both the shopper and the commercial merchandising sector are needed.[1]

For a change in productivity, we are interested in the reduction in resources needed to achieve a particular outcome. For example, if the retail and wholesale sectors remain unchanged, but shoppers become more informed and obtain greater value from the spectrum of services offered by that sector, productivity has increased. Resources are freed for other purposes. One of the achievements of broader-based education, for example, may be an extension of the breadth of the market by expanding the buyer's knowledge of his or her rights and options in a transaction.

By and large, only anecdotal evidence exists for the inputs provided by consumers, and even less evidence exists on how consumer inputs to shopping have changed over time. One notable exception to the absence of consumer shopping input data in Canada is provided by the eight-volume Canadian Time Use Pilot Study. From this study we know, for example, that Canadian households in 1981 spent approximately 45 minutes each day in shopping activities.[2] Unfortunately, intertemporal comparisons can be made only with the 1971 Halifax Panel Study. Now that this type of analysis has begun in Canada, we recommend that the continuing collection of this type of information be regularized. Ideally, one would like to be able to match the time-use information with the other household information collected in the census.

The exclusion of the inputs provided by the shopper also makes it possible to draw false conclusions on the more narrowly focused question of whether resources are being used more efficiently in the commercial sector. For example, a measurement that indicates that the same amount of food is being sold through more stores employing more clerks does not necessarily mean that food shopping has become less efficient. That conclusion could be drawn only if it were known that driving costs, the costs of holding inventories in freezers, and the selection time spent by the shopper did not decrease to offset the additional resources absorbed within the organized trade sector.[3] If the stores were providing more convenient locations and packaging, their costs would be rising and the margin they charge would increase. A measure of store output that concentrated on the margin, rather than on the amount of food passing through the store, would then appropriately reflect an increase in output. The substitutability of the inputs provided by the shopper and the trade sector can cause some productivity measures of the trade sector based on some output measures to give misleading signals.

Technical change in the commercial trade sector that reduces the inputs needed from the shopper provides another example where false inferences can be made by failing to consider that shopping is co-produced by the shopper and the merchant. For example, consider a change in a display or checkout practice that permits a food store to save time for its shoppers. Assume also that no additional costs are incurred to make these changes. Since customers will choose stores that reduce their shopping time, stores are driven by competition to introduce these changes. In the new equilibrium that results, real sales will be the same as before, gross margins will be the same as before, and the inputs into the commercial sector will be the same as before. Measured productivity will be unchanged in the trade sector, but that sector has initiated changes which have resulted in a resource gain to the economy.[4]

OTHER CONCEPTUAL ISSUES IN MEASURING PRODUCTIVITY

The Bundling of Characteristics

An output measure for the trade sector should indicate whether the bundle of characteristics valued by the shopper and provided by the trade sector has risen or fallen. The bundle of characteristics will include: the quality of goods purchased, the parking arrangements, the convenience and attractiveness of its location and opening hours, the aesthetic environment, the information provided by the personnel, by advertising, and by the display of merchandise, et cetera. When a customer makes a purchase, all of the attributes are purchased in a bundle. In equilibrium, the value of the bundle must equal or exceed the money paid, which in turn must equal or exceed the cost of providing all of the components. However, this is not true for each component separately. One shopper may not require "free" parking, and another may be tone-deaf and not appreciate the quality of the sound system playing the background music. These shoppers will value particular characteristics below their marginal cost. For the bundle to be purchased, however, the other characteristics must be valued at more than their cost at the margin. For some characteristics (like parking) shops can, and many do, price the service separately, but for other characteristics separate pricing would be prohibitively expensive.

Unpriced Outputs

An important aspect of the provision of shopping services is potential free-riding. Some customers consume valuable services and do not pay at all. For a customer who looks over the goods, gains information from the sales personnel, listens to the music, and socializes with other customers but does not buy, a value is created that leaves no statistical trace. On average, the sales of the outlet have to cover the costs of providing these services to the "window-shoppers." The services are paid for, but not necessarily by those who consume them.[5] Because of free-riding, these services will be provided in smaller amounts than would be the case if there were some mechanism for charging those who actually benefit.

Competition for the Marginal Shopper

If shoppers do not record through separate transactions the value they derive from the provision of parking, atmosphere, product information, or the returns policy of the store, how do market forces influence a store or wholesaler's choice of these attributes? The spatial character of competition provides a clue to the answer to this question. Consider a situation where shoppers buy a particular set of goods and a store that offers the most attractive package of distribution services to these shoppers. With its current choice of location, environment, informational policies, display layouts, opening hours, average queue lengths, and pricing strategy, the store's customer base will include some shoppers who derive economic rents from the quality-price choice of the store.[6] The store is so convenient or the amenities valued so highly that some shoppers would still make their purchases at the store if it charged them a membership fee. Other shoppers, however, are on the margin between making their purchases at that store and making them at another outlet. It is the latter group, the marginal shopper, which is the focus of competition among existing stores.

In these circumstances, a store will tailor its quality-price choice to attract additional shoppers. The inframarginal shoppers will be affected by this competitive response and may have their economic rent altered by it. As long as inframarginal customers continue to enjoy some surplus from shopping at that store, the store's sales to them will be unaffected by the change in strategy. Any change in their surplus is irrelevant to the profit-maximizing choice of the store. It is then conceivable that total sales of a store, and its profits, may rise, but there is a more than offsetting fall in the surplus of the inframarginal customers. In circumstances where some of the strategic choices of the store have public goods attributes (e.g., location, opening hours, and environmental variables) and the characteristics are bundled together and sold at the same price to any purchaser of a good, competition will not ensure that the quality-price mix is the value-maximizing one.[7]

This aspect of spatial competition results from economies of scale and scope in merchandising. If each person had his or her own store with its characteristics tailored to that individual's tastes, no inframarginal customers would exist in equilibrium.[8] This discreteness is reinforced by economies of scale in the use of the shopper's time from doing all one's shopping in one location. There is a cost to the customer of combining the characteristics of many stores by making a number of distinct shopping trips. Together these factors generate the existence of individuals who earn rents from the merchandising decisions of stores.

Consequences for Productivity Measures

Output measures are always aggregates of disparate elements. An economically meaningful way of adding together disparate components is to give each component a weight dependent on its value to consumers. Where each component is priced, the marginal valuation of each consumer will be equated to the price, and the price then becomes the appropriate weight.[9] For the reasons outlined above, competitive retailing and wholesaling are characterized by customers who earn rents from the offerings of the outlets from which they purchase goods. This phenomenon presents difficulties for the interpretation of productivity statistics, as illustrated by the following example.

Consider a situation in which a store caters to neighbourhood customers who walk to the store. Perceiving that it will be profitable to expand its customer base, the store initiates "free parking" and raises its margin to cover these costs. Assume that the neighbours who walk to the store continue to do so after prices have risen. As new shoppers with cars shift their custom to the store, the quantity of sales will rise. Neighbourhood shoppers, on the other hand, pay more for their goods without receiving any additional services that they value. Profits rise, as do aggregate sales, reflecting the higher value to the mobile customers, but local customers are harmed by the change. The increment in sales weighted by the prices takes no account of the damages and therefore provides a distorted view of real output and productivity.

Available Output Measures

The real output measures that are available are real sales, the deflated margin, and real value added. Real retail sales are calculated by deflating nominal sales by a price index.[10] The resulting series provides an accurate index of output for the trade sector if the characteristics provided by the seller are proportionate to real sales.

The other two output measures are derived from the input-output statistics. The deflated margin is the real measure of gross output for the trade sector in the Canadian input-output system. It is the difference between real sales and the real cost of goods to the trade sector. Nominal value added measures the nominal margin less the cost of services bought by the trade sector from other sectors, such as lighting and heating. Real value added is the nominal value added deflated by a double deflation process. Whether either of these concepts represents units that are a meaningful output measure for a productivity calculation depends on a number of factors.

Neither the deflated margin nor real value added have a concrete physical counterpart; there is no physical entity that can be weighed or otherwise measured. The use of aggregates, however, is common both in economics and in everyday language. Labour, capital, utility, and information are examples of economic aggregates that are commonly referred to and none of these has a homogeneous physical counterpart. However, to be useful for productivity calculations an output aggregate must meet quite stringent conditions.[11] It is unlikely that any of the available output measures can be used to calculate meaningful productivity trends for the trade sector without extreme caution. Denny and May have argued that the necessary conditions for value added to be a meaningful measure of output for Canadian manufacturing do not hold.[12] No studies have come to our attention concerning the validity of these assumptions for the retail or wholesale sectors. With manufacturing, the problem is less acute because the measure of gross output for each industry in the input-output table is unaffected by these considerations. For the trade sector that is not true, since it is treated differently in the table and its gross output is the deflated margin. This measure is conceptually similar to value added.[13]

Calculating Productivity Ratios

The denominator in a productivity ratio can be either a measure of one type of input, such as the amount of labour, or a measure of all the factors. The latter ratios are called multifactor productivity ratios. Some measures take a simple ratio of output to an input aggregate; others take an output and derive the net inputs required to produce it through calculations made with the Canadian input-output table. In the latter approach there are different techniques for attributing the productivity change between sectors.[14] In the following section we report the results of two recent studies on productivity and calculate a number of simple productivity ratios.

MEASURES OF TRADE SECTOR OUTPUT PER INPUT UNIT

Current Measures of Trade Sector Productivity

To illustrate the differences that can arise in the measurement of productivity within the trade sector, we consider the results of two recent studies in Canada. The first is a 1986 study, by G. Stuber, of productivity growth between 1975 and 1983. The labour productivity measure used is the contribution to GDP by the sector (i.e., real value added is the output measure) divided by sector employment.[15] Stuber's calculations for labour productivity over the whole time period, as well as over the business cycles (measured from peak to peak), are presented in table 4 below.

Table 4
Stuber's Measures of Labour Productivity Growth

Output/Employee	1975–83	66Q1–69Q4	69Q4–74Q1	74Q1–79Q4	79Q4–81Q2
Manufacturing	1.6%	3.5%	4.3%	1.4%	0.2%
Trade	0.4%	−0.2%	3.4%	0.1%	−0.5%

Source: Gerald Stuber, "The Slowdown in Productivity Growth in the 1975–83 Period: A Survey of Possible Explanations," *Bank of Canada Technical Report 43*, The Bank of Canada, Ottawa, October 1986, pp. 11 and 14.

In terms of Stuber's labour input measure, the trade sector has had a slower rate of growth than manufacturing in all time periods since 1966. Moreover, the trade sector has experienced only one period of sustained productivity growth since 1966, and that was confined to a brief three-year period from 1971 to 1973. Since then, productivity has remained roughly constant despite relatively high rates of growth in real output (2.8 percent) at the very end of Stuber's time period.[16]

An alternative set of productivity measures is calculated by T. K. Rymes and A. Cas. Using real output as employed in the input-output tables to derive a measure of multifactor factor productivity, Rymes and Cas calculate the annual percentage rates of growth of multifactor productivity by year for 37 different industries.[17] The results for the trade sector, using both Hicksian and Harrodian measures, are presented in table 5.[18]

Table 5
Rymes and Cas' Measures of Total Factor Productivity
Annual Percentage Average Rate of Growth in the Trade Sector

	1972	1973	1974	1975	1976	1977	1978	1979	1980
Hicksian MFP	4.01	2.16	0.38	−0.97	3.95	−2.15	−0.90	1.03	−1.38
Harrodian MFP	5.05	3.49	0.02	−1.30	5.00	−2.16	−0.84	1.88	−1.19

Source: T. K. Rymes and A. Cas, "New Canadian Measures of Multifactor Productivity," *On The Feasibility of Measuring Multifactor Productivity*, Statistics Canada, Winter 1985, chapter VIII, tables 4.0.1 and 4.0.2, pp. 31 and 33. [Also, forthcoming Cambridge University Press.]

While the Rymes and Cas figures are measures of total factor productivity, the general message conveyed is the same as Stuber's. That is, productivity seems to have increased rapidly in the early seventies and stayed roughly constant throughout the rest of the seventies.[19] The year-to-year measures of this table show a pattern of annual variation that averages close to zero.

Real Sales per Input Unit

While the Stuber study and the study by Rymes and Cas are relatively recent, both studies end in the early eighties in a time period that coincides with and is dominated by the 1981–82 recession. To give a more up-to-date picture of developments in the trade sector, we present a number of different output-to-input ratios that may place a better perspective on the period of the late seventies.

In figure 11, real (1971) sales per trade employee are presented on a monthly basis between 1972 and 1985, while in figure 12 the annual figures for real (1971) sales per unit of the net capital stock are plotted. The monthly series of figure 11 are both seasonally adjusted and unadjusted to illustrate the large variation in this measure that arises due to the bunching of sales over the Christmas season. The time pattern exhibited in the two figures is remarkably similar and in neither figure is there much evidence of a time trend.[20] Real sales per employee per month varied about $1,900 (1971) per month over this time period, while real sales per unit of capital appear to be returning to the $4,500 (1971) per annum figure that began the time period. The conclusion arising from these measures of trade productivity is then consistent with that suggested by Stuber, although the extension of his series through 1986 would indicate a continuing period of growth since 1983.

Real sales per employee and per unit of capital have varied similarly over the business cycle. Both measures suggest that the trade sector responded in only minor ways to variations in real levels of economic activity prior to the 1981–82 recession. Both measures peaked in 1976, bottomed in 1982, and showed similar percentage swings over the downswing of the cycle.[21]

Real Value Added per Input Unit

Changes in the value of real retail sales reflect activities in the economy as a whole. Real value added, on the other hand, is designed to measure only the marketing sector's output, that is, the distinctive output that is combined with both shoppers' inputs and the goods and services provided by the rest of the economy to "produce" the shopping activity. By identifying nominal

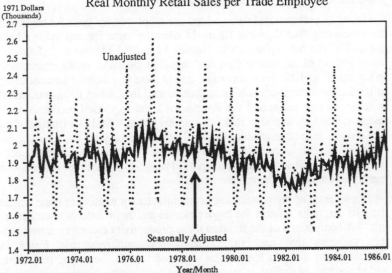

Figure 11
Real Monthly Retail Sales per Trade Employee

1971 Dollars
(Thousands)

Unadjusted

Seasonally Adjusted

Year/Month

Source: CANSIM, D656069 and D772006.

Figure 12
Real Retail Sales per Real Unit Capital

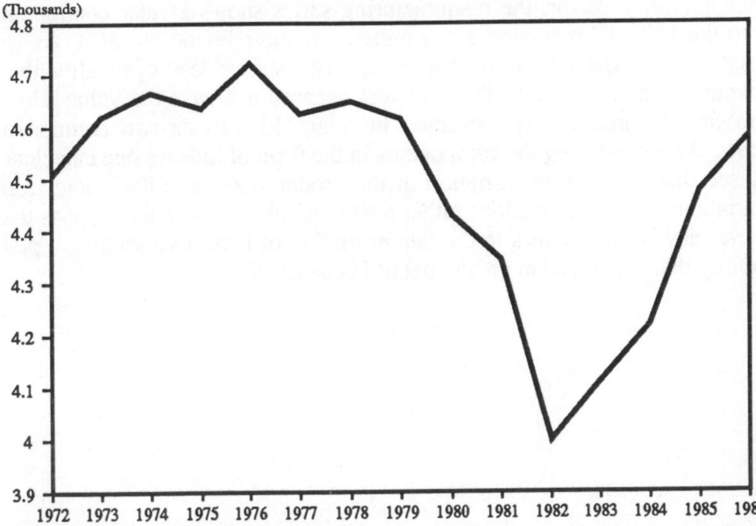

1971 Dollars
(Thousands)

Source: CANSIM (13-211) D656069, D883278.

and real output measures that reflect the resources used in the trade sector, performance can be documented and assessed.

Figure 13 presents real value added per employee for both the trade and manufacturing sectors, while figure 14 does the same for real value added per unit of the net capital stock. Figures 13 and 14 present a slightly different pattern of movement than the "sales" productivity series represented in figures 11 and 12. With real value added there is a definite upward trend in labour productivity, much more pronounced than when it was measured in terms of real sales, and the downward trend in capital productivity is reversed when measured in real value added terms.[22] Stuber's finding of no real change in labour productivity is illustrated nicely by the virtual constancy of the employee ratio in trade between 1976 and 1981. The perspective given by seeing the entire time period suggests that this episode may be merely a plateau in a longer time trend.[23]

The reversal of the positioning of manufacturing relative to trade across the two diagrams reflects the higher capital-to-labour ratio in manufacturing.[24] A comparison of the trend in these productivity measures across sectors suggests that real value added per employee rose faster in manufacturing than in trade.[25] In terms of capital, however, real value added per unit of capital in manufacturing declined both relative to that in trade and in absolute terms.[26] In the trade sector, the two real value added to input measures grew in tandem, while the same ratios in manufacturing moved in opposite directions.

Taking into account the upward trend of labour productivity in the manufacturing sector, the manufacturing series shows greater contraction into the 1981–82 recession and a more dramatic rebound out of it. As we might have expected from chapter 2, trade shows less cyclicality than manufacturing. Figure 15 is of interest because it breaks the value added measure of productivity presented in figure 13 into its two component parts. By representing the components in the form of indexes one can clearly see that most of the variation in the productivity ratio has come from variations in real value added rather than in employment. This suggests that there may be differences in the labour market of these two sectors, a possibility that is pursued in greater detail in chapter 4.

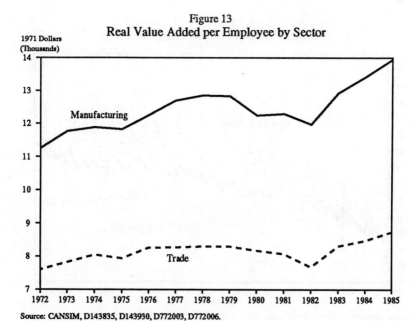

Figure 13
Real Value Added per Employee by Sector

1971 Dollars
(Thousands)

Manufacturing

Trade

1972 1973 1974 1975 1976 1977 1978 1979 1980 1981 1982 1983 1984 1985

Source: CANSIM, D143835, D143930, D772003, D772006.

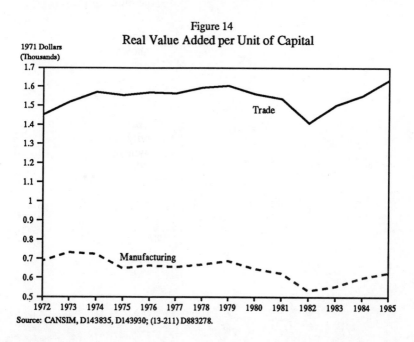

Figure 14
Real Value Added per Unit of Capital

1971 Dollars
(Thousands)

Trade

Manufacturing

1972 1973 1974 1975 1976 1977 1978 1979 1980 1981 1982 1983 1984 1985

Source: CANSIM, D143835, D143930; (13-211) D883278.

Figure 15
Real Value Added and Employment
(1971 = 100)

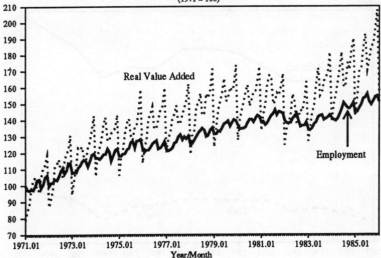

Source: CANSIM, D144446 and D772006.

NOTES

1. Shopping, S, may be viewed as being produced by the inputs of the buyer, represented by a vector B with arguments of shopper's informational capital, shopper's time, shopper's capital (such as automobiles), et cetera, and the outputs of the trade sector, represented by the vector T which has the arguments: spectrum of goods offered, information provided, financing services available, implicit guarantees, and the like. This multi-dimensional vector T is produced by L, K, and M, where L is a vector of the different types of labour hired by the trade sector, K is a vector of capital services, and M is intermediate inputs. Written as functions, $S = S(B,T)$ and $T = T(L,K,M)$.

2. Appendix B, "Number of Minutes Spent Per Day by All Respondents and Participants on All Primary Activities Collapsed to 99 Codes, for Each Community," in Brian L. Kinsley and Terry O'Donnell, *Marking Time: Explorations in Time Use, Volume 1,* Employment and Immigration Canada: Ottawa, 1983. The figure quoted in the text comes from the sum of categories 30 to 39 in table 4 on page 37.

3. Note that changes in the number or size of stores (and hence capital expenditures on buildings) and changes in the number of employees (and hence employee time) are direct substitutes for the travel time and expense of the customer. Because productivity measures typically exclude customer-provided inputs, the change in the productivity measure captures only one part of the change in shopping. Moreover, it will result in incorrect prediction of the direction of productivity change whenever the increase (decrease) in sector-provided resources is smaller than the resource saving (expenditure) by the consumer.

4. Another way of viewing the change is that the real output of the trade sector has risen and inputs have not, but none of the traditional measures of output of the trade sector (real sales, deflated margin, or sector value added) will capture that increase in output. This other perspective is discussed later in this chapter.

5. The purchasing consumer is "taxed" and the window-shopper is "subsidized" in the present system of organization.

6. We will refer to the choice along all the relevant dimensions by the store as the quality-price choice.

7. See, for example, A.M. Spence, "Monopoly, Quality and Regulation," *The Bell Journal of Economics,* (Autumn 1975), 417-29, and J.S. Fer-

ris, "Time, Space and Shopping: The Regulation of Shopping Hours," Working Paper, November 1987.

8. Even with scale and scope, if the characteristics provided by stores were limited in number, and the population density were sufficient, the set of characteristics might be spanned by the variants offered by stores of the minimum efficient size. For some characteristics a customer could then choose a mix which reflected his or her tastes accurately. Unfortunately, the location dimension is infinite in the sense that each customer is uniquely located with respect to the configuration of stores.

9. The appropriate measure of the proportional change in output of a group of components is then the sum of the proportional change in each component weighted by the value share of that component in the total value of the components. This records the change in what is called a Divisia index.

10. Presumably, the statistical agency does its best to deal with the classic index number problems in choosing a deflator. The deflation index must account for the fact that: (a) existing products are constantly being improved in quality; (b) new products are constantly being introduced; and (c) the composition of products in aggregate sales is constantly changing as incomes, prices, age profiles, and information sets change.

11. In principle there are two ways that nature could co-operate to make real value added and deflated margin meaningful as a sector output measure. The production function for trade services must be able to be written as $T=T(f(g(K,L),M^*),M^{**})$ where L is the labour and K is the capital of the trade sector, M^* is the vector of purchases of services from other sectors that are not offered for resale, and M^{**} is the vector of goods that are bought from manufacturers and resold. The f function relates to the deflated margin and the g function relates to value added. [Cf. K. J. Arrow, "The Measurement of Real Value Added" in P. A. David and M. W. Reder (eds.) *Nations and Households in Economic Growth* (Academic Press 1974) for the discussion with respect to value added. The argument is exactly the same for the deflated margin.] The second condition is that both the T function and the f function exhibit constant returns to scale with respect to their arguments. The third condition is that the marginal revenue from buying more goods, materials, and services from other sectors be equal to their price. [For a detailed discussion of the three conditions see Kazuo Sato, "The Meaning and Measurement of the Real Value Added Index" *Review of Economics*

and Statistics (1977).] When all of these conditions are met, a unique value added index can be calculated, through a double deflation process. A second way in which nature could co-operate to make real value added a useful economic measure of output is if the prices of all inputs purchased from other sectors moved in parallel with the output prices of the sector. [Cf. W. E. Diewert, "Hicks' Aggregation Theorem and the Existence of a Real Value-Added Function" in chapter III.2 of M. Fuss and D. McFadden, *Production Economics: A Dual Approach to Theory and Application* (North-Holland 1978) p. 41. From the continuity of the function, Diewert suggests that if prices had moved approximately proportionately, empirical research that assumed a production function in real value added would be warranted.]

If these measures are used for productivity purposes, a further restriction must be imposed on the evolution of the production process over time. Technical change in each sector must augment the factors used in the sector, and productivity increases in other sectors could impact only through the prices paid for their output.

12. Ibid., p. 66.

13. Because, for example, the shirt bought from the manufacturer is in fixed proportion to the sale of the shirt, the necessary separation to justify deflated margin is more credible than that for value added.

14. The Harrodian and Hicksian techniques are discussed and contrasted in the study by T. K. Rymes and A. Cas, *On the Feasibility of Measuring Multifactor Productivity* (Cambridge University Press, forthcoming), chapter 8, New Canadian Measures of Multifactor Productivity.

15. Gerald Stuber, "The Slowdown in Productivity Growth in the 1975–83 Period: A Survey of Possible Explanations," *Bank of Canada Technical Report 43*, The Bank of Canada; Ottawa, October, 1986.

16. Stuber, p. 47.

17. The input-output measure of the real output of the trade sector is the gross trading margin (where the gross margin is measured as real sales minus the real cost of the good acquired from the manufacturing sector). This differs from Stuber's measure of real output by including in its definition the real resources provided by sectors other than those supplying the product that is being resold.

18. Harrodian measures adjust all produced inputs for the changes in efficiency in their industry of origin, whereas Hicksian measures do not.

19. It is also interesting to note that the same pattern of movement (but not the level) is revealed by both the Hicksian and Harrodian measures.

20. There is a very slight upward trend to retail sales per employee and a similarly small downward trend to real sales per unit of net capital. It seems likely that the recovery from the 1981–82 recession is not complete in the time period covered by these graphs.

21. The percentage decrease in real sales per employee between 1976 and 1982 was 12.5 percent while the decrease for real sales per unit of capital was 13 percent.

22. Between 1972 and 1985, the growth in output per employee in trade is 15 percent when measured in terms of real value added and 3 percent when measured in terms of real sales.

23. It is also worth reporting the calculations of Sharpe who acquired data on total actual hours worked from the Labour Force division of Statistics Canada. Because of the downward trend in hours worked through time, the measure of productivity in these terms would be expected to be higher than in terms of the number of employees. The average real (1971) value added per hour worked in retail, wholesale, and manufacturing, in the five-year periods prior to 1985 was:

	1975-80	1981-85
Retail	0.50%	1.23%
Wholesale	1.50%	2.99%
Manufacturing	0.90%	2.62%

Source: Sharpe (1986) as reported in H. Grubel and M. Walker, *The Canadian Services Industries*, The Fraser Institute, (forthcoming 1988), table 6.1, p. 87.

24. Note, however, that the analysis of chapter 4 points to the greater use of part-time labour in the trade sector. Because both measures use the total number of employees, part of the observed gap between real value added per employee and its trend through time may represent different trends in hours worked and/or part-time employment. That is, differences may arise from imprecise measurement.

25. Real value added per employee grew by 24 percent in manufacturing as opposed to 15 percent in trade over this 13-year period.

26. Real value added per unit of capital contracted by 9 percent in manufacturing, while the same measure grew by 13 percent in trade.

Chapter 4

LABOUR MARKET CHARACTERISTICS

INTRODUCTION

The last two chapters depict the "service" output of the trade sector as displaying less variability than the "goods" output of the manufacturing sector. Relative to manufacturing, the trade sector seems to have been able to absorb the real shocks affecting the economy through price rather than quantity adjustments. The evidence also shows that in the trade sector employment has both less seasonality and less cyclical variation than in manufacturing. This suggests that there may be differences in the characteristics of labour used in the service sectors. Finally, our earlier work also points to a closer connection in the variability of the wholesale and manufacturing sectors than between wholesale and retailing. This chapter investigates the characteristics of the workers employed in these sectors with a view to seeing whether some of these sectoral differences can be explained in terms of the characteristics of the work force or the organization of that market.

To structure our discussion we focus on the measurability issues associated with rewarding labour productivity. The first part of the chapter uses the demographic detail made available each decade in the census to attribute earnings differentials across sectors to differences in demographic characteristics. The second part of the chapter explores in detail a more topical issue. Observed wage and/or earnings data in Canada indicates that women earn less than men on average, and the inability to attribute this difference to measurable "economic" factors has resulted in legislation designed to close this gap. Our analysis uses a more detailed sociological data base in an attempt to isolate more fundamental reasons for this differential.

AGGREGATE LABOUR CHARACTERISTICS OF
THE TRADE SECTOR

In this section we use census data to examine a number of demographic characteristics of the labour force in the wholesale and retail trade sectors. The fact that there is something interesting to discuss is suggested not only by the observations described above but also because employee earnings in the trade sector differ from those in other sectors of the economy. The analysis of this chapter is then organized as an investigation of the earnings differentials within this sector and between it and the rest of the economy.

Average Weekly Earnings in the Trade Sector

The trade sector has a reputation for generating jobs with relatively low earnings. This is confirmed by the data. Table 6 reports average weekly earnings in trade and manufacturing for each of the years between 1983 and 1986. As that table illustrates, average weekly earnings in the trade sector were slightly more than 60 percent of earnings in manufacturing. Even after adjusting for the smaller number of hours worked, weekly earnings in the trade sector remained substantially lower.

While earnings in the trade sector as a whole are lower than those in manufacturing, there is a similar earnings gap within the trade sector. Figure 16 plots the average weekly earnings of employees in the retail sector against the average weekly earnings of employees in industry as a whole and in the wholesale and manufacturing sectors. This provides additional support for the contention that the wholesale sector exhibits characteristics that distinguish it from the retailing industries.

In the census year of 1981, the average weekly earnings in the retail sector were between 60 and 68 percent of those earned by employees working in the wholesale sector (within the same province across Canada).[1] Average weekly earnings in wholesaling were only marginally (between 88 percent and 97 percent) lower than those earned in manufacturing. In both cases this differential was larger than it was in 1971. In that year, average weekly retail earnings were between 70 and 80 percent of wholesale earnings, while average weekly earnings in wholesaling were virtually identical to those in manufacturing. It follows that both across provinces and over time there has been a persistent difference in earnings among the retail, wholesale, and manufacturing sectors, and the differential appears to have increased over time.[2]

The persistence of the earnings differential over time suggests that it should be explainable in terms of the equilibrium characteristics of the workers and/or industry. Some of the reasons that have been advanced as the cause of this differential are: differences in the education and skills of

Table 6
Average Weekly Earnings and Hours Worked

	1983	1984	1985	1986
Average Weekly Earnings:				
Trade	$282.77	$293.64	$304.28	$317.50
Manufacturing	$440.67	$465.66	$488.17	$504.04
Trade Percentage of Manufacturing	64%	63%	62%	63%
Weekly Hours Worked:				
Trade	28.7	29.0	28.9	28.9
Manufacturing	38.4	38.5	38.8	38.7
Hours Adjusted Trade Earnings *	$378.34	$391.18	$408.51	$425.16

Source: Statistics Canada, "A Review of Employment and Earnings Data, 1983-1986," *Employment, Earnings and Hours*, 72-002, June 1987.

Note: * Calculated as average weekly earnings divided by trade weekly hours times manufacturing hours.

Figure 16
Average Weekly Earnings by Sector

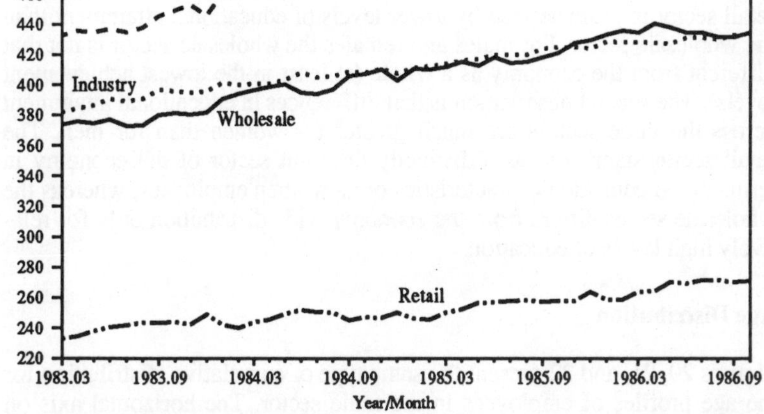

Source: CANSIM (8007) L1241, L1267, L1437, L1456.

sector employees, differences in the average age and related job experience of those employees, and differences in the attachment of employees to the work force in this sector (for example, a desire for part-time versus full-time employment). Finally, it is sometimes argued that the low wages arise in retailing because the retailing sector has a relatively large proportion of women. Each of these possibilities is considered in turn before their joint contribution to observed earnings differentials is investigated.

Education Background

Figures 17, 18, and 19 present the education profile of employees in the trade sector versus those in the economy as a whole. The education classes in the cumulative distributions are the percentage of the labour force with *less than*: (a) grade 9, (b) some high school, (c) a high school diploma, (d) some technical training after a high school diploma, (e) some university, (f) some university together with technical training, or (g) a university degree.[3] As is apparent from figure 17, where the distribution for the trade sector as a whole is compared with the labour force as a whole, the trade sector utilizes employees with lower levels of education on average than does the rest of the economy. About 60 percent of the work force in trade has an education level equal to or below a high school diploma, while this percentage is closer to 50 percent for the labour force as a whole.

Figures 18 and 19 present the education profiles of the retail and wholesale sectors separately for both men and women. There are two interesting features in these diagrams. First, on both diagrams the cumulative distribution for the retail sector is higher than either the wholesale sector or the labour force as a whole. This means that while levels of educational attainment are lower in the trade sector than in the economy as a whole, the retail sector is characterized by lower levels of educational attainment than the wholesale sector. For males and females the wholesale sector is not that different from the economy as a whole (at least in the lowest achievement levels). The second observation is that differences in educational attainment across the three sectors are much greater for women than for men. The retail sector stands out as a distinctly different sector of the economy in terms of the education characteristics of its women employees, whereas the wholesale sector differs from the economy-wide distribution only for relatively high levels of education.

Age Distribution

Figures 20, 21, and 22 present the same type of cumulative distribution for the age profiles of employees in the trade sector. The horizontal axis on each of these diagrams shows the age groups (15 to 19 years, 20 to 24

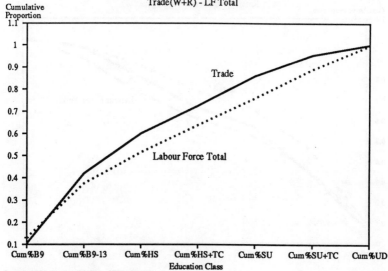

Figure 17
Education Profile: Aggregates 1981
Trade(W+R) - LF Total

Source: 1981 Census (93-961...973) table 16.

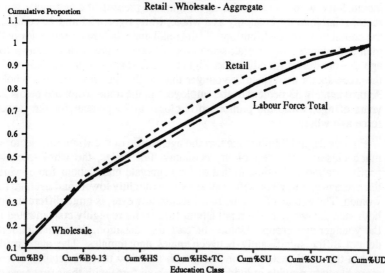

Figure 18
Education Profile: Males 1981
Retail - Wholesale - Aggregate

Source: 1981 Census (93-961...973) table 16.

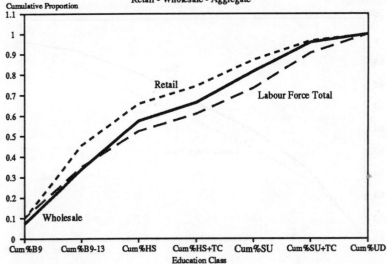

Figure 19
Education Profile: Females 1981
Retail - Wholesale - Aggregate

Source: 1981 Census (93-961...973) table 16.

years, and so on), while the vertical axis measures the proportion of the labour force with *less than* this age. Figure 20 presents the aggregate trade sector relative to the economy as a whole, while figures 21 and 22 compare the cumulative age distributions for the retail and wholesale sectors for both men and women. In general, same types of conclusions can be drawn for age as were drawn for education. Figure 20 illustrates that the employees in the trade sector are typically younger than in the labour force as a whole. Approximately 33 percent of the employees in the trade sector are below 25 years of age, while the proportion is closer to 25 percent for the labour force as a whole.

Figures 21 and 22 illustrate that the age profile of the wholesale sector is much closer to the rest of the economy. For males, the wholesale age profile is almost identical to that of the aggregate male labour force, while the average age in wholesaling appears to be slightly lower than average for women. The age profile in the retail sector, however, is quite different. For both men and women, the retail labour force is more highly concentrated in the younger age groups. Unlike the case for education, these distributions do not differ significantly between males and females. The age profile within the retail sector is consistent with the view that the retail sector is more likely to provide individuals in the labour force with their first taste of work experience.

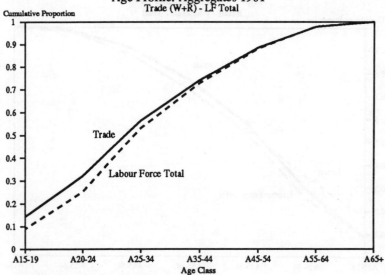

Figure 20
Age Profile: Aggregates 1981
Trade (W+R) - LF Total

Source: 1981 Census (93-961...973) table 16.

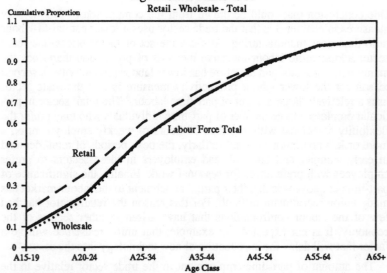

Figure 21
Age Profile: Males 1981
Retail - Wholesale - Total

Source: 1981 Census (93-961...973) table 16.

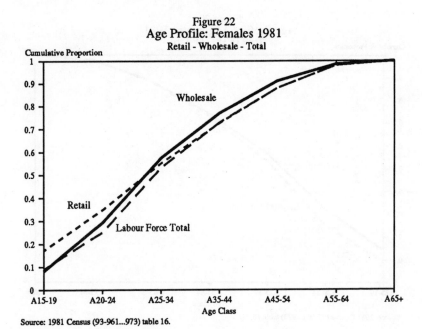

Figure 22
Age Profile: Females 1981
Retail - Wholesale - Total

Source: 1981 Census (93-961...973) table 16.

Part-Time Employment

One conclusion that could be drawn from the comparison of productivity
measures in chapter 3 is that the trade sector uses a lower capital-to-labour
ratio than does manufacturing. At the same set of factor prices, the retail
sector adopts more labour-intensive methods of production than does the
manufacturing sector and therefore has lower labour productivity. A second
reason for the lower labour productivity measure is that the trade sector
uses a relatively large amount of part-time labour.[4] The retail sector in particular employs a large number of part-time individuals who may prefer the
flexibility associated with less than 30 hours of weekly employment on a
more or less continuous basis. Similarly, the peak periods of retail demand
in early summer and late fall lead employers in these sectors to prefer
employees with preferences for seasonal work. Finally, the significance of
part-time employees is that their partial attachment to the labour market has
made union recruitment difficult. For this reason the retail sector has had
few of the labour confrontations that have arisen in other sectors of the
economy. It is not expected, for example, that union resistance will be a
factor that will delay the introduction of new technology into the sector.[5]

The amount of part-time employment in the trade sector relative to the
economy as a whole is illustrated in table 7 below.

Table 7

**Part-Time Employment as a Percentage of Full-Time Employment
by Industry, Occupation and Sex, June 1981 (January 1987)**

Industry/Occupation	Both Sexes	Male	Female
All Industries	14.6 (20.4)	6.0 (9.5)	30.2 (38.1)
Manufacturing	3.3 (3.6)	1.7 (1.8)	7.7 (8.4)
Trade	26.7 (33.3)	12.3 (17.0)	52.4 (63.6)
All Occupations	14.6 (20.4)	6.0 (9.5)	30.2 (38.1)
Sales	23.3 (35.6)	8.9 (17.7)	55.8 (67.2)
Services	36.8 (56.0)	18.6 (34.3)	55.7 (78.3)

Sources: Statistics Canada, *Labour Force Survey*, 71-529, p. 51; Statistics Canada, *The Labour Force*, 71-001, January 1987, table 31, p. 58.

Note: "Part time" consists of persons who usually work less than 30 hours per week and consider themselves employed part time.

As table 7 illustrates, part-time employment in the trade sector is disproportionately important. In 1981, for every 4 full-time employees in the trade sector, 1 was part-time. The corresponding ratios for industry as a whole and manufacturing were 1 in 8 and 1 in 33. While the percentage in part-time employment has varied for men and women in roughly the same way across all sectors (less in trade than in all, but more than in manufacturing), part-time employment occurs much more frequently for women than for men. In the trade sector, there was 1 woman part-time for every 2 women working full-time (versus 1 in 8 for men). The corresponding number for women in manufacturing is 1 in 12 (1 in 50 for men). The concentration of women in part-time shopping employment is also indicated by occupation data. Occupations such as sales and services figure prominently in both female employment and the percentage who work part-time. As the table also illustrates, the importance of part-time employment has grown. In 1987, all of the above categories have higher part-time employment percentages. This is part of a longer-term trend that has been influencing the labour markets since the middle seventies.[6]

Sex

The single most important demographic characteristic of the labour market in the period since the Second World War has been the dramatic growth in the participation of women in the labour market. Table 8 presents the time trend of these figures for the census years 1951, 1961, 1971, and 1981. In the 30-year period covered by this table, female participation has quad-

Table 8

Distribution of the Canadian Labour Force in Total
and in the Trade Sector by Sex and Census Year

	1951	1961	1971	1981
Total Labour Force	5,286,407	6,471,850	8,626,925	12,054,245
Male	4,123,270	4,705,510	5,665,715	7,155,355
Female	1,163,137	1,766,332	2,961,210	4,898,890
Female Percentage of Total	22%	27.3%	34.3%	40.6%
Total Trade	745,617	997,336	1,269,290	1,997,096
Percentage of Total Labour Force	14.3%	15.4%	14.7%	16.6%
Male	540,981	694,211	803,100	1,132,660
Percentage of Total Male	13.1%	14.8%	14.2%	15.8%
Female	213,636	303,125	466,190	864,436
Percentage of Total Female	18.4%	17.2%	15.7%	17.6%
Percentage Female in Trade Total	29%	30%	37%	43%

Sources: 1971 Census of Canada, *Industries*, 94-739, vol. III; 1981 Census of Canada,
    93-961 . . . 973, table 16.

rupled while the male labour force less than doubled. In relative terms, the
female proportion of the labour force doubled from 22 to 41 percent by
1981. The table also shows that the trade sector participated in the growth
of female participation (female trade employees rose from 29 to 43 percent
of total trade employment).

On the other hand, the trade sector has not become any more or less important as a source of employment for women. In 1951, 18 percent of the
female labour force was employed in the trade sector; by 1981 that figure
had again returned to 18 percent. If anything, trade employment has
declined as a source of jobs for women as it has increased in importance for
men. The trade sector has always been an important source of jobs for
women participating in the labour force; however, its relative importance to
women has not increased through time.

Labour Market Characteristics and Average Weekly Earnings

In this section the variables discussed above from the 1971 and 1981 census are used to attempt to account for the variations in average weekly
earnings that have arisen across industries and across provinces in Canada.
This was done by running a multiple regression equation in which all of
these variables were used to explain average weekly earnings. Theoretical
considerations lead us to predict that average weekly earnings will be lower
in those industries and provinces that use employees with lower levels of

education and younger age distributions, and that rely more heavily on part-time employment. In addition, differences in provincial labour market conditions can be expected to influence provincial weekly earnings. The prediction is that higher unemployment rates will be reflected in lower average weekly earnings.

With this background, the regressions for 1981 (including the variable for part-time) and 1971/81 (excluding it) are presented in table 9 of appendix I to this chapter. The regressions show that the inclusion of the part-time variable leads to a significant improvement in the ability of the regression to predict variations in average weekly earnings across industries and provinces. The joint hypothesis embodied in the regression equation that includes the part-time variable accounts for over 90 percent of the variation in average weekly earnings in 1981, while the equation accounts for 78 percent of the variation over the two census years 1971 and 1981 after including dummy variables for the year and the retail sector.

Somewhat more importantly, all the individual characteristics discussed above appear as significant determinants of the earnings differential across industries and provinces. Age, education, and variable representing part-time differences all appear with the expected (negative) sign and are significantly different from zero, both age and part-time at the standard 5 percent significance level. Similarly, average weekly earnings do respond to the particulars of provincial labour markets. The provincial unemployment rate is significantly negative in its effect on average weekly earnings.

Finally, the female proportion of the employed labour force appears consistently in regressions of this type as having a negative effect on earnings. That is, after adjusting for observed differences in the age and education distribution and for differences in the use of part-time employment, higher proportions of females in the industry's labour force will result in significant reductions in average weekly earnings. Why this occurs is not explained by our data. The census data does not allow us to connect an individual's sex with age, education level, and/or choice of part-time versus full-time employment. To answer these questions we need data centred on individuals and their job choices. This type of data is available in the Carleton Social Sciences Data Archives. It is to this data that we now turn.

WOMEN IN THE LABOUR FORCE OF THE TRADE SECTOR

As the statistics presented earlier in this chapter indicate, women have entered the labour force in unprecedented numbers. Changing lifestyles and dramatically lower fertility rates have combined with changes in the perception of appropriate gender roles to alter the educational and occupational choices of women. In the process, these social and economic changes have placed considerable pressure on our institutions to adapt. The trade sector has played an important role in the adjustment that has already occurred, and it can be expected to both participate in and be strongly influenced by ongoing developments in this area.

Although our institutions have responded in ways that have permitted us to realize much of the potential in this revolution of social attitudes, there is a continuing concern that women are being discriminated against in the job market. The evidence, as indicated by the earlier regressions and by other statistical analyses, is that women do get paid less. Historically, women have participated differently from men in the work force in general and the trade sector in particular. For example, in describing Toronto's retailing practices during the 1860s, William Stephenson notes:

> A male clerk earned four or five dollars a week to start, rising perhaps to $10 after five years. Females normally started at no pay, but received $2.50 per week if they proved themselves over a six-month probation period. Office or cash-boys and message runners started at a dollar a week, or less.[7]

The same author also reports that marriage at Eaton's was often an expensive adventure for a woman, at least if she could not keep a secret.

> If a female employee married, she was expected to resign to give a job to a married man with children. Eatonians who married each other sometimes kept the fact a secret for years to avoid loss of the second pay cheque.[8]

The size and the cause of the earnings gap between men and women have been the focus of much current research. In this section we (a) outline a number of different hypotheses of how an earnings gap might arise; (b) discuss briefly a statistical procedure for estimating the gap; (c) apply that method to a micro database to compare the sensitivity of earnings to gender in the retail and wholesale sectors with that in the rest of the economy; (d) discuss the relevance of these results, and similar exercises done by others, to identifying causes of the earnings gap; and (e) assess the policy options for reducing any of the difference attributable to discrimination.

Hypotheses for Why Women Are Paid Less Than Men

Economic theory predicts that competitive labour markets reward workers according to the value of their contribution to output. Thus before an earnings gap can be attributed to other influences on the wage structure (such as gender), account must be taken of measurable factors affecting productivity, such as differences in employees' experience, training, apprenticeships, education, and hours worked. If a residual earnings gap then arises and can be related to gender (or some other measurable characteristic of workers), a number of hypotheses compete to explain this phenomenon. One possibility is that market arrangements reflect prejudice, resulting either in unequal pay for the same job or in job segmentation. Explanations not based on prejudice have also been articulated.

Explanations Based on Prejudice

Hypotheses of gender prejudice which would result in a discriminatory wage gap in labour markets include:[9]

(a) Employers are willing to forgo profit in order to hire a man over a more productive woman because they are prejudiced.

(b) Employers are not prejudiced, but male employees are, so that production actually falls when women are added to the team.

(c) Women are socially harassed in jobs where they work with men and thus choose to work in lower paying "women's" occupations in order to avoid the harassment.

(d) The job market is stratified into women's jobs (inferior jobs) and men's jobs (superior jobs) and reinforced by the sex-stereotyping behaviour of parents, teachers, and the media.

(e) Women are employed by discriminating monopsonistic employers who reduce the earnings of women employees by exercising their market power.[10]

Economic Explanations Not Based on Prejudice

Among the economic arguments explaining the earnings gap that don't depend on gender discrimination are the following:

(a) Employers have been and remain uninformed about the true productivity of women.

(b) Women are not as well informed about opportunities in the labour market as men.[11]

(c) Women have a taste for the non-pecuniary aspects of certain types of employment and this results in employment segmentation. The phenomenon is not driven by discrimination but rather by the relative scarcity of jobs with these characteristics.

(d) Differences in wages reflect some unmeasured differences in attributes or behaviour between men and women.

The Statistical Measurement of the Earnings Gap

Statistically, the earnings received by any individual can be related to the attributes of the individual, the employer, and the job. Some of the attributes that affect the productivity of the individual are acquired, others are discretionary, and still others are innate. Among the acquired attributes that have been singled out for attention are education, experience, marriage, and on-the-job training. Examples of discretionary attributes are intensity of effort, degree of commitment to the work force, and the degree of "opportunism" shown by the employer and the employee. Among the characteristics that are innate or reflect cultural conditioning are ethnic background, religious beliefs, and physical characteristics such as size, dexterity, and gender.

Similarly, differences in earnings might be expected if the employee was self-employed or, if not, if the employer was a government, a non-profit organization, or a commercial enterprise. Size of establishment may also affect productivity. The net value of work done may depend on the region in which the job is located or on whether the job is in a rural or urban setting.[12] Unionization may also affect wages.

The variables listed above are merely suggestive of the types of variables that have been tried. Each empirical study is restricted by the information contained in the data set on which it is based.[13] In addition, all studies are limited to quantifying the effects of variables that can be measured. Some factors such as hours worked or years of education may be readily measurable, while others like intensity of effort or degree of opportunism are inherently difficult, if not impossible, to measure.[14]

After accounting for as many of the measurable factors as data and degrees of freedom permit, the discrepancy in earnings between men and women is reduced considerably, but almost all modern statistical studies of earnings find that a significant difference remains. Canadian studies, for example, indicate that the unadjusted ratio of female to male earnings is approximately 60 percent.[15] Taking account of education, experience, hours worked, training, location, occupation, and industry increases the ratio to the 75 to 85 percent level. If comparisons are made within the same occupation and the same establishment, the ratio rises to the 90 to 95 percent level.[16] These studies have been done over different data sets, and include cross-sectional and combined cross-section and time series tests. Similar results have been found for studies done in the United States.

An analysis of trade sector earnings based on census data has already been provided, but only some of the effects of potentially measurable influences can be examined using the census data. Through the Social Science Data Archives at Carleton University, access was obtained[17] to the Comparative Class Structure Project (CCSP) database, which contains a significant amount of information gathered by interviews with a representative sample of Canadians for 1983.

Earnings Equations Based on the CCSP Data Base

To examine whether the determinants of labour earnings in the trade sectors differ from those of other sectors in the Canadian economy, we ran some regressions on the data.[18] The dependent variable was the natural logarithm of earnings.[19] Explanatory variables that reflected training, experience, education, effect of living in a city, and unionization were included. One set of variables was included to capture regional effects; another was entered to measure any shifts in the relation due to industry effects. A variable for unionization and one for urban respondents were added. Hours worked were taken into account, as were the expressed commitment[20] of the employee to staying in the labour force. A variable was included to measure whether living with a wife or partner affects male earnings. Finally, a set of variables measuring the impact on earnings of being a woman living alone as compared to living with a husband or partner and whether the impact of education or experience differed if the employee was a woman were added.

A First Look at the Data

The first regression grouped the data for all industries.[21] The hypothesis being tested assumed that the effects of age, education, experience, commitment, and so on were independent of the industry in which the individual was employed. The impact of the industry was then limited to a shift in the intercept of the relationship. The variables used in the regression equation and the values of the estimated coefficients and derived statistics are reported in detail in table 10 in appendix II to this chapter. The coefficients for experience, years of school, hours worked, urban residency, commitment to staying in the labour force, and unionization all have their expected sign and are statistically significant.[22] For a worker earning the sample mean income[23] of almost $17,000 per year, the following effects on income are indicated: living in a city increases income by $3,036; expressing commitment not to leave the work force raises income by just over $2,000; acquiring an additional year of education adds $1,302; adding an additional year of experience increases income by $280. Those who were unionized earned $2,237 more than those who were not.

At the mean income of the sample, a male's income rises by over $4,700 per year if he lives with a wife or partner rather than living alone. This coefficient captures the gender effect in this sample since the set of female variables[24] does not add significantly[25] to the explanatory power of the independent variables. The same is true for the set of regional variables[26] and the set of industry variables.[27]

What Is Different About the Trade Sector?

The preceding regression did not reveal any significant difference in the earnings relationship for the trade sector. The possibility of an industry effect, however, was limited by the presence of a single shift parameter. By running separate regressions for the retail, wholesale, and "other" industries, the coefficients for each variable can vary across each grouping. There were 41, 24, and 433 observations, respectively, in the three industry groupings.[28] A comparison of the sample means for selected variables in the sample is provided in table 11. Because the small number of observations for the wholesale sector makes inferences for that sector questionable, the regression results for wholesale are reported in appendix II but are not commented on in the text. The comparison between the results for the retail and the other industries, however, is illuminating.[29]

For both the retail and "other" industries category, the experience and years of schooling variables were significantly positive in their effect on earnings, while the variables for apprenticeship and job-specific training were insignificantly different from zero. For a person earning the average income in each sector, an additional year of experience increases income by $506 in retail and $264 in other industries. Retail differs from the "other" industry category in the insignificance of hours worked, city living, and unionization as determinants of income.

The retail sector differs dramatically from the "other" industries sector in the importance of the commitment variable. Commitment is not a significant determinant of earnings in the retail sector,[30] but it is both positive and highly significant in other industries. The evidence is consistent with the view that jobs in the retail sector have not penalized those who anticipate periods of time when they will leave the work force. This feature of retail jobs makes them particularly attractive to individuals who want to work intermittently (or on a permanent part-time basis) because of family or other responsibilities.

In the sample, the coefficients of the set of female variables are not significantly different from zero in either sector. Nevertheless, there is an interesting difference in gender effect revealed by the regressions. The coefficient of the male living with wife or partner variable is *not* significant in retailing but is highly significant in the other industries. In the "other" industries regression, a male living with a wife or partner makes $4,930 more than a male living alone who, in turn, earns the same average income as the group. This evidence is consistent with the married male group not receiving a premium wage in the trade sectors.

Table 11
Sample Means

Variable	Wholesale	Retail	Other
Income			
— for everyone	$19,653	$15,321	$16,932
— for men	$22,697	$18,583	$20,131
— for women	$12,708	$11,968	$14,045
Years of Education			
— for everyone	11.79	11.61	12.65
— for men	11.78	11.26	12.75
— for women	11.83	12.06	12.55
Years of Experience			
— for everyone	22.63	19.35	17.61
— for men	25.61	20.65	18.20
— for women	13.67	18.11	16.96
Proportion Unionized			
— for everyone	.13	.05	.41
— for men	.17	.09	.46
— for women	0	0	.34
Hours Worked			
— for everyone	38.94	37.00	37.11
— for men	42.52	40.45	40.45
— for women	29.96	32.79	33.78
Proportion Committed			
— for everyone	.83	.83	.75
— for men	.83	1.00	.87
— for women	.83	.61	.62

Source: Sample drawn from *The Comparative Class Structure Database*. See Appendix II for more detail.

This result may be related to our findings for commitment. One explanation for the existence of a married male premium is that employers infer additional information on commitment from an applicant's status as married and male.[31] In our sample, for example, cohabitation status provides different information for men than for women. For instance, the simple correlation between the logarithm of hours worked and cohabitation is markedly different for men than for women. Men who lived with their wife or partner worked longer hours than other men, while women with the same domestic situation worked fewer hours than other women.[32] If employers inferred the strength of commitment from domestic status and sex for jobs for which commitment was important, a male living with a wife or partner would command a higher wage. This effect should disappear if the revolution in gender roles makes the classification carry little differential information on commitment.

What Explains the Gender Gap?

The *statistical significance* of gender-specific variables, in our case the significance of a male living with a partner or wife, provides no information on the *cause* of the earnings gap. The interpretation of statistical findings depends in large part on the prior beliefs that one brings to the study. Those who believe that prejudice pervades the labour market, for example, can interpret these results as supportive of their views (married males gain at the expense of those who are discriminated against) as can those who believe in non-discriminatory causes (such as the commitment interpretation given above). Similar problems of interpretation arise in studies that examine the effect of ethnic or religious background on earnings.[33] When a group of variables that measure the effect of membership in a particular religious group is found to have a significant effect on earnings, a researcher must seek to interpret the findings in terms of the additional information on the religion and society before deciding whether discrimination or some other factor is the cause.[34]

Further guidance for the interpretation of our results can be derived from a closer examination of the data in table 11 and the consistency of competing interpretations with the data that is available. At the time that our data was gathered, men (on average) had acquired more of the measurable determinants of productivity and had made more of the discretionary decisions that generated higher earnings. Men had more experience, were more committed to employment, and typically worked longer hours. If, in addition, the unmeasured attributes of productivity that can be acquired are important and, like the measurable attributes, have been accumulated more by men than by women, the credibility of attributing at least part of the residual gap to productivity differences is increased.

The Importance of Unmeasured Attributes

The inability to measure all job attributes can lead us to misinterpret the significance that is attached to those variables that are measurable. The difficulty of quantifying all the attributes and characteristics that generate value in a job (and the arbitrary nature of measurement if subjective evaluation is quantified) is illustrated by an American study done by Raisian, Ward, and Welch.[35] These authors refer to the U.S. Labor Department's assessment of 12,000 job classifications in terms of 46 different characteristics, many of which are nebulous at best. One such category is "people."

For this job characteristic, the evaluator is asked to rank between 0 and 8. The instructions state that an 8 means "taking instructions or helping," where helping refers to "non-learning helping" when no "variety of responsibility is involved." A 0, on the other hand, is given if "mentoring: dealing with individuals in terms of their total personality in order to advise, counsel, and/or guide them with regard to problems that may be resolved by legal, scientific, clinical, spiritual, and/or other professional principles" is undertaken. Other types of categories receive different numerical ranges and are often given similarly vague guidelines.

Even if unmeasured productivity attributes and differences in the commercial value of educational choices were accounted for, however, there would still likely persist a gap that reflects lags in the adjustments to dramatic changes in social attitudes on the part of larger institutions' behavioural codes and practices. What is the appropriate social response to the remainder attributable to prejudice?

Policy Options

Equal Pay Regulation

One response to the possibility of discrimination is to regulate the labour market. The scope of regulation can vary from measures intended to ensure equal pay for equal work to broader approaches aimed at equal wages for work of equal value. Equal pay for equal work legislation exists at both the federal and the provincial level. In 1956, the federal government passed the Female Employees Equal Pay Act,[36] which requires the same pay for employees doing the same or similar work in an establishment. Equal pay for equal work within an establishment is also covered in specific provincial legislation or in the general anti-discrimination provisions of provincial human rights legislation.[37] Under some of the legislation, remedial action occurs in response to complaints, while under others a complaint procedure is augmented by routine investigations by the relevant labour department. If a case is brought, and several have been, settlement or judgement may involve the payment of millions of dollars in back pay to employees who have not been paid according to the requirements of the law.[38]

The equal pay for equal work laws have not satisfied those who seek a legislative solution to the earnings gap. Indeed, since the gender earnings gap for the same occupation within the same establishment has been found to be in the 5 to 10 percent range, one Canadian expert in this field has concluded that there is "rather limited scope for equal pay for equal work legislation in closing the earnings gap" and that there is "a larger scope for affirmative action in equal pay for work of equal value legislation."[39]

Comparable-Worth Regulation

In 1978, the Federal Government extended its wage regulation to cover equal pay for work of equal value. Quebec has done the same under its Charter of Human Rights and Freedoms, and Ontario recently passed Bill 154, An Act to Provide for Pay Equity.[40] A brief consideration of the Ontario legislation will illustrate the nature of this legislative approach, and its potential impact on the trade sectors.

Comparable-worth legislation provides for female-dominated job categories to be paid equivalently to male-dominated job categories within the same establishment. Criteria for determining an establishment, dominance and equivalence, for permitting exemptions, and for defining appropriate remedies have to be established and are crucial to the impact of the legislation. An appropriate administrative and enforcement structure must also be developed.

In Ontario, an establishment refers to all of the employees in a geographic division.[41] Firms with less than 10 employees are exempted. Those with 10 to 99 employees do not have to develop a "plan," although they may still be subject to complaint if the objectives of the bill have not been accomplished. Part-time employees are not counted in determining the size of an employer. In its submission to the Consultation Panel on Pay Equity, the Retail Council of Canada opposed exemptions based on size, because they would "discriminat[e] against medium-sized and larger employers who would be subject to pay equity legislation."[42] In contrast, the Canadian Federation of Independent Business, which has many small retailers and wholesalers among its members, advocated a general exemption for small businesses.

If the effective dividing line becomes firms with more than 100 employees, less than half of the retail sector will be covered by this legislation. If the evidence reported here is supported in further studies, i.e., if gender is not a significant determinant of earnings in retail, consideration should be given to exempting the retail sector *in toto* from the provisions of this and similar bills.

In the Ontario legislation, differences in pay resulting from the following practices are excluded from consideration: seniority, merit, red-lining, and bargaining strength.[43] Merit is an understandable exemption, but it is difficult to understand why seniority and bargaining power are exempted. Is it the case, for example, that the discrimination of the old and established over the young and those with little bargaining strength is any fairer than gender discrimination?

Red-lining permits an employer to freeze the wages of employees who have been downgraded in the process of adjusting to changed circumstances. One of the uses of red-lining is likely to be in implementing the remedies of the legislation. The wage increases paid to successful plaintiffs must be financed from somewhere, and since capital is mobile in the long run, the incidence of these awards must fall on the real wages of other groups. The Green Paper issued before the legislation was passed stated that reductions in wages to satisfy the requirements would not be permitted. Adjustment will apparently come by freezing the money wages of those who have not been granted positive increments, until the general upward drift of money wages brings the structure of real wages sufficiently into line.

In deciding whether a job will be classified as a male or a female job class, Bill 154, section 1(5) states that "regard shall be had to the historical incumbency of the job class, gender stereotypes of fields of work and such other criteria as may be prescribed by the regulations." A job class must have similar duties and responsibilities as well as similar recruiting procedures and compensation schedules. Once classifications have been made according to these vague guidelines, a more precise criterion is imposed to determine whether the class is gender-dominated or not. Job classes are female if they contain 60 percent or more women; they are male if they contain 70 percent or more men.

In providing guidance for determining work of equal value, Bill 154 is equally Delphic. Equal value refers to "... a composite of the skill, effort and responsibility normally required in the performance of the work and the conditions under which it is normally performed." One pamphlet released by the government asks the question "How can the value of a secretary's job be compared to that of a groundskeeper's?" and provides the following answer:

> While a secretary's job may involve better working conditions than a groundskeeper's, her job could require more responsibility, effort and skill. If that's the case, the overall value of the secretary's job class could be the same as the groundskeeper's and she should be paid the same.[44]

Unfortunately, it also might not be the same. To actually decide requires an ability to quantify the criteria and attach weights to the score on each.[45]

The difficulty of actually doing this can again be illustrated by the Raisian, Ward and Welch study. These authors found that four aggregated attributes captured most of the variation in the total scores of each job classification. These were "substantive complexity, motor skills, physical demands and undesirable working conditions." Skill and working conditions are common to this set and the criteria proposed under the Ontario law. It is instructive to consider the ratings of physicians, elementary school teachers, registered nurses, aircraft mechanics, hairdressers, and carpenters for each of these four characteristics. These are given in table 13.

Table 13

U.S. Labor Department Rating Characteristics

Occupation	Characteristic Levels*				Percent	Hourly
	(1)	(2)	(3)	(4)	Female 1982	Wage 1981
Physicians	8.6	9.9	0.8	0.0	15.1	15.87
Elementary school teachers	6.2	3.6	1.0	0.0	80.1	9.38
Registered nurses	6.1	6.6	1.0	0.0	94.9	8.73
Aircraft mechanics	5.1	7.1	5.2	0.1	2.0	10.76
Hairdressers and cosmetologists	5.1	9.2	0.0	0.0	90.9	4.80
Carpenters	4.7	7.0	8.4	0.1	1.8	8.05

Source: J. Raisian, M. P. Ward and F. Welch, "Pay Equity and Comparable Worth," *Contemporary Policy Issues*, April 1986, p. 10.

Note: * The four characteristics are (1) substantive complexity, (2) motor skills, (3) physical demands and (4) undesirable working conditions.

Interesting comparisons can be made between doctors and nurses, and between elementary school teachers and carpenters. Are male carpenters unfairly treated in the market in comparison to female elementary school teachers? Given the attributes involved, why are aircraft mechanics paid such a substantial premium over carpenters?[46] Whatever the causes of these differences, the table highlights the fact that choosing criteria, translating them into measures, and suitably weighting them will be a focus of much conflict, debate, and lobbying effort.

What the ultimate impact of the new Ontario legislation will be is not clear. The number of workers affected under the federal comparable-worth legislation has been estimated at 0.3 percent of the total covered, and an even lower figure proportion has been estimated for the Quebec legislation. On the other hand, similar legislation in the state of Washington affected 35 percent of the covered workers.[47] Depending on assumptions made about the number of workers affected and the adjustment in the wages of these workers, Gunderson has estimated the direct cost of the program to be between $15 and $7.8 billion, with the most likely outcome being between $1 and $3 billion.[48]

These figures concentrate on the magnitude of the transfers involved and do not address the economic cost in terms of the reallocations of capital and labour or a reduced organizational response, an important area of innovation in the trade sectors. Some other predictable effects of this law on the retail and wholesale sectors are: (a) the encouragement of the hiring of more part-time labour; (b) the expansion of small firms which are "subsidized" by being exempted from this legislation and the contraction of large firms which are "taxed;" (c) an increased amount of subcontracting from the affected large-firm sector to the uncovered portion of the economy; (d) shifts in the terms of some labour contracts to emphasize elements of the wage package which are overvalued in the bureaucrats' formulas for aggregating fringe benefits and the wage into one total; (e) increased female unemployment; and (f) additional paperwork and other administrative burdens.

Although the direction of these effects is predictable, the size of the effects is not known at present. If the labour market is made "fairer" by these changes, this benefit may easily outweigh the costs generated. A civilized society should be prepared to incur costs to root out prejudice. The extent to which this legislation does that will be revealed over time. A final concern of the authors is that it is preferable to write anti-discrimination laws so that they cover all disadvantaged groups, and not just one targeted subset. By permitting specific legislation, non-disadvantaged groups are encouraged to use political power to redistribute income in their favour under the guise of instituting targeted anti-discrimination regulation.

Markets and Discrimination

Markets provide safeguards against discrimination. In a competitive economy, owners who wish to discriminate against women must pay a price for so doing. Their wage bill is larger (or output smaller) than it needs to be, and profits are less. This does not mean that these firms will not survive; only that owners must "spend" some of their income to indulge their prejudices. In areas like retailing, customers increase the implicit "tax" being paid by prejudiced employers by buying their products and doing shopping in stores where the staff's composition suits them. If a majority of customers are prejudiced, then the problem is more acute, but political institutions in this setting are less likely to counter discrimination than economic ones.

If prejudice arises from the labour force (rather than from the employer), the market will reward a neutral manager who hires either all men or all women working teams. This is because a gender-homogeneous labour force is more productive. There is no reason why in this setting all women production teams should earn less than all men teams. If all women teams were as effective but less expensive to hire, all gender-neutral managers would attempt to hire them and in the process drive their wages back up. Of course the market in which a service is sold may not be indifferent to the sex of the seller or even the producer, but endemic prejudice among buyers calls for a very different response than regulating the labour market.

If, instead, the problem is the managers' ignorance of the true productivity of women, then competition from more-informed rivals will tend to drive poorer managers out of business or at least force them to bear the costs of their ignorance. If remedial action by the state is required, the logical policy is either to inform store managers of how they can make greater profits by changing their hiring practices or to inform store owners so that nonlearning managers who cost them profits can be replaced. The dissemination of information, however, is costly. A possible rationale for threatened state regulatory action and/or symbolic action by the state is to force employers to think about the rationality of their hiring decisions.

A variant of the information problem concerns statistical discrimination. If the average woman either performs or chooses differently in the labour force than does the average man and employers do not have reliable information on the individual applying, employers will have a commercial incentive to infer attributes about the individual from their knowledge of the average for the group. In many cases this does the individual a disservice, and the fact that it is efficient on average often provides little or no comfort. One of the purposes of anti-discrimination labour regulation will be to prevent the use of this type of information when it runs counter to the equality of opportunity. The tentative evidence from our regressions is that in the retail sector, sex and domestic status are not being used as conditioning variables in determining earnings.

Finally, some of the hypotheses explaining the cause of the earnings gap depend on monopsonistic or monopolistic power. At this time, we are unaware of any important barriers of this type in the retail and wholesale occupational groups, but, if there are any, competition policy should be brought to bear.

It is not surprising that the dramatic changes in gender roles should cause friction within existing institutions and spawn new governmental responses. It would be a shame, however, if the less-visible process by which present institutions adapt or new private organizations are introduced is restricted unnecessarily by government initiatives. It takes time and is costly for internal behavioural and hiring codes to evolve within large public and private organizations. However, as long as men and women can start their own firms to capitalize on innovative groupings and organizational structures, existing institutions will be under increasing pressure to address present practices. Since the disciplining force of organizational change is the market response when established institutions are slow to react, threats to its vitality may appear more than usually abstract when compared to the other costs of wage regulation. Reliance on market forces may also seem merely a veiled way of defending the status quo. Quite the opposite is true, however. As the following chapters discuss, organizational innovation has been a integral part of the evolving history of the trade sector and a vital part of its contribution to economic progress and constructive change in Canada.

NOTES

1. Average weekly earnings were collected from Statistics Canada, *Employment, Earnings and Hours*, 72-002, table 2. The numbers discussed in the text for 1971 and 1981 were collected for the month of June. This was to use earnings data that coincided as closely as possible with the date of the collection of the census data on labour market characteristics.

2. Note that from figure 16, average weekly earnings in wholesale averaged 85 percent of those in manufacturing over the past 4 years.

3. The data for the education profiles in this subsection, and the age profiles in the next, come from the 1971 and 1981 census: for 1971, 94-740 volume III, table 2, and for 1981, 93-(961...973) table 16 for male and female.

4. Because the labour productivity measure in chapter 3 uses the total number of employees, the measure of productivity will be biased downward compared to a measure that uses full-time-equivalent employees.

5. The Ontario Task Force on Employment and New Technology, *Appendix 17, Employment and the New Technology in the Retail Trade Industry*, Toronto: Ontario Government Publications, 1985, food stores, pp. 28-30; general merchandise stores, pp. 56-59. It is true that there is an incentive for employers to hire part-time employees in order to avoid unionization and perhaps to avoid some of the pension and other obligations that need to be met with full-time employment. That incentive exists for manufacturers and employers in other sectors as well. What is clearly indicated by the data is that the retail sector has a comparative advantage in making productive use of people who wish to work on a part-time basis.

6. From 1976 to 1985 part-time employment has increased by 67.8 percent, compared to 13.3 percent in full-time employment. See Maryanne Webber, "Labour Market Developments in Canada: 1986," *The Labour Force*, Statistics Canada (71-001), p. 102.

7. W. Stephenson, *The Store that Timothy Built* (McClelland and Stewart 1969), p. 14.

8. Ibid., p. 95.

9. The seminal work on the economics of discrimination is G. S. Becker, *The Economics of Discrimination* (University of Chicago Press, 1957).

Among those making important contributions are K. J. Arrow, "Models of Discrimination" and "Some Models of Race in the Labor Market" in A. H. Pascal (ed.) *Racial Discrimination in Economic Life* (Lexington Books 1972), A. Kruger, "The Economics of Discrimination" *Journal of Political Economy* 71 (October 1973) and B. Bergmann, "Occupational Segregation, Wages and Profits When Employers Discriminate by Race or Sex" *Journal of Political Economy* (March/April 1971).

10. If the employer has monopsonistic power in both the male and female labour pools, the elasticity of supply of women would have to be lower than that for men for women's wages to be lower in equilibrium.

11. One empirical study of women executives in the United States concluded that "who you know" was very important in the salary game:

    ...managerial women need more than larger corporations and greater human capital investments to be successful. In order to make the most of their opportunities and human capital investments, women need to be plugged in to networks that provide requisite labor market information.

    Robin L. Bartlett and Timothy I. Miller, "Executive Compensation: Female Executives and Networking" *American Economic Review* 75 no. 2 (May 1984) p. 270.

12. Monopsonistic labour markets are more likely in a rural or small town setting.

13. For an excellent summary of work done in Canada see M. Gunderson and Frank Reid, *Sex Discrimination in the Canadian Labour Market: Theories, Data and Evidence,* (Women's Bureau of Labour Canada, March 1981) and M. Gunderson, "The Male-Female Earnings Gap in Ontario, A Summary" Employment Information Series No. 22 (February 1982) *Research Branch Ontario Ministry of Labour.*

14. Creative thinking is one example, which is why an R&D lab is so difficult to manage effectively.

15. In answer to the question: "Why is Pay Equity Necessary?," a Manitoba government document states:

    Pay equity is necessary to reduce the wage gap between men and women. On average, women only earn $0.66 for every $1.00 men earn. [*The Facts on Pay Equity,* published by the Minister of Labour

and the Minister Responsible for the Status of Women for the
Government of Manitoba. p. 1.]

Unfortunately that ratio by itself provides limited information.

16. See M. Gunderson, "The Male-Female Earnings Gap in Ontario: A
Summary," Employment Information Series No. 22 (February 1982)
Research Branch Ontario Ministry of Labour, p. 17.

17. We are grateful for the generous help of Wendy Watkins of the Social
Science Data Archives.

18. Although we were as careful as possible, the results should be considered with the extreme caution that should be standard in judging
empirical work. Details of the regression results are provided in appendix II of this chapter.

19. Earnings do not include fringe benefits. For a discussion of the possible importance of fringe benefits see M. Gunderson and Frank Reid,
*Sex Discrimination in the Canadian Labour Market: Theories, Data
and Evidence*, (Women's Bureau of Labour Canada, March 1981) pp.
51-54.

20. Commitment has been found to be a significant factor in earnings functions. For a Canadian study that focuses on controlling for differences
in commitment by comparing single men and women over thirty, see
Roberta Robb, "Earnings Differentials Between Males and Females in
Ontario, 1971," *Canadian Journal of Economics* (May 1978).

One American study reports that "after 16 years out of school, women
average only half as much labor market experience as men," and "a
typical young woman who entered the labour market in the early 1970s
worked only six of the next ten years." J. Raisian, M. P. Ward, and F.
Welch, "Pay Equity and Comparable Worth," *Contemporary Policy Issues* (April 1986) p. 14. These commitment differences are reflected in
the falling ratio of remuneration at different age levels. They estimate
that with the same continuity the gap between earnings of men and
women would be halved.

The commitment of employees affects the calculus of whom to train in
skills that are specific to a job. Large firms do more on-the-job training
than small. It would be credible that they favour those who were expected to be more committed to the workplace than those who were
not. Traditionally men were more committed. The following evidence
reported by Walter Oi is consistent with this view: "Wages of men in

large firms were 54 percent higher than wages of men in small firms; the differential was only 37 percent for women." W. Y. Oi, "Neglected Women and Other Implications of Comparable Worth," *Contemporary Policy Issues* (April 1986) p. 28.

21. The primary sector was excluded from all the regression results.

22. The specific training variable has a negative coefficient. The training should increase earnings after it has been completed and lower them before completion.

23. Since the dependent variable is the natural log of earnings, the coefficients of the qualitative independent variables provide multiplier effects on income. Therefore the dollar change depends on the base income.

24. Female living alone, female living with a husband or a partner, female interacting with education, and female interacting with experience.

25. If all the coefficients for the set being introduced were actually zero, one would observe the F value for the change or a higher one 33.91 percent of the times as a result of sample variation.

26. If all the coefficients for the set being introduced were actually zero, one would observe the F value for the change or a higher one 35.11 percent of the times as a result of sample variation.

27. The adjusted R squared fell with the addition of the industry variables.

28. The actual regression equation is presented in table 12 in appendix II of this chapter.

29. Because of the small number of observations for the wholesale and retail sectors, the regional variables which individually and as a group were not significant in the "all industry" regression were dropped. See table 12 in appendix II of this chapter.

30. The coefficient estimate of commitment is actually negative in the retail sector, but in any case is not significantly different from zero at the usual levels of significance. The coefficient estimate is positive for wholesale and although not significant from zero at the customary 95 percent level, it is at the 90 percent level.

31. The question on which the commitment variable was calculated was "Since you began working ...was there ever a time when you did not have a job, and did not want to find a job." It is unlikely to be a sufficient statistic for information on commitment. An uncommitted new

entrant or an employee who was not committed but had not yet inter-
rupted his or her employment would not respond "yes" to this question
and would be registered as committed.

32. For the three industry groups, the correlations for women (men in
brackets) are -.801 (.359) in wholesale, -.461 (.421) in retail, and -.308
(.278) in the other grouping.

33. The American situation is reported in B. Chiswick, "The Earnings and
Human Capital of American Jews" *Journal of Human Resources*, 18
(Summer 1983). The Canadian data are analysed in some excellent
work by Nigel Tomes, "Religion and the Rate of Return on Human
Capital: Evidence from Canada," *Canadian Journal of Economics*, 16
(1983), and "The Effects of Religion and Denomination on Earnings
and the Returns to Human Capital," *Journal of Human Resources*, 19
(Fall 1984). Some additional interesting evidence is provided in R.
Meng and J. Sentance, "Religion and the Determination of Earnings:
Further Results," *Canadian Journal of Economics*, 17 (1984).

34. For example, one robust result of work on ethnic and religious effects
on earnings is that Jewish males make more than non-Jewish males,
ceteris paribus (see, for example, P. Kuch and W. Hessel, *An Analysis
of Earnings in Canada*, Statistics Canada, 1979). Most observers
familiar with Canadian and American societies would deny that institutions are biased in favour of Jews. Anyone who did believe that would
then have difficulty explaining why the same institutions are apparently biased against Jewish women. A recent study showed that Jewish
women earn less than their female counterparts in other religious
groups. (See N. Tomes, "Religion and the Earnings Function,"
American Economic Review, May 1985.) A host of forces may be
responsible for the joint phenomenon. For instance, it is credible that in
the Jewish culture over the period reflected in the data, Jewish women
spent time and resources reinforcing their spouses' careers and incomes at a cost in terms of the money earned in their own careers.

35. J. Raisian, M. P. Ward, and F. Welch, "Pay Equity and Comparable
Worth," *Contemporary Policy Issues* (April 1986).

36. Its provisions have since been included in the Canada Labour Code.

37. Ontario moved its equal pay provisions from the Human Rights Act to
the Employment Standards Act in 1968.

38. Some examples are cited in Labour Canada, *Equal Pay Legislation and Implementation: Selected Countries* (Labour Canada, August 31, 1984).

39. M. Gunderson, "The Male-Female Earnings Gap in Ontario: A Summary," Research Paper n. 22, Ontario Ministry of Labour, February 1982, p. 12.

40. Chapter 34 Statutes of Ontario, 1987. Manitoba also has such legislation, requiring the civil service, crown agencies, and "external" agencies (hospitals and universities) to evaluate jobs in a gender-neutral manner and to raise the pay of "dominated classes."

41. For example, a county, regional municipality, or the municipality of Metropolitan Toronto.

42. The Report of the Consultation Panel on Pay Equity, p. 25. The position of the Retail Council is developed in detail in Retail Council of Canada, *Bill 154: An Act to Provide for Pay Equity in the Broader Public Sector and in the Private Sector, Submission to the Ontario Legislature's Justice Committee* (February 1987).

43. If a female category is not unionized, comparison is restricted to a male category within the same establishment which is not unionized. Only where such a comparison cannot be made can union and nonunion earnings be used in a comparison.

44. Ontario Women's Directorate, *Questions & Answers, Pay Equity in the Workplace*, p. 14.

45. In a document called *The Facts on Pay Equity*, published by the Minister of Labour and the Minister Responsible for the Status of Women for the Government of Manitoba, the following is included in an answer to the question "Can you compare jobs which are as different as apples and oranges?":

> Here's one way it can work. Point factor systems assign points for the skill, effort, responsibility and working conditions involved in each job. The points are then added to determine the relative worth of the jobs. When the state of Minnesota used this approach, it found, for example, that a Clerk typist IV position was comparable in value to a Grain Inspector II. (p. 2.)

There is no information given on how many grain inspectors would equal one Minister of either title. The Pay Equity Bureau in the

Manitoba Ministry of Labour has published a 68-page guide to *Job Analysis and Job Description*. The complexity of just this part of the task is reflected in the ten pages providing a glossary of terms presumably required to read the rest of the document. Manitoba's Pay Equity Bureau is aware of the problems. The package of information that they sent to us included an excellent set of warnings about the difficulties, in a paper written by Gene Kiviaho and titled "Rating Bugs & Biases." As they attempt to implement their Pay Equity Act they will discover some solutions to these problems and undoubtedly create some new ones.

46. Discrimination does not appear credible as an explanation, and we suspect that unmeasured factors are the cause.

47. Figures are from M. Gunderson, *Costing Equal Value Legislation in Ontario* (Ontario Ministry of Labour, 1984) pp. 2.21 to 2.24.

48. See M. Gunderson, *Costing Equal Value Legislation in Ontario* (Ontario Ministry of Labour, 1984), table 8.1 and surrounding discussion. Gunderson does not quantify but does mention indirect costs resulting from the impact on men's wages.

APPENDIX I

Average Weekly Earnings Regressions for 1971 and 1981 Census Years

Before reporting the regression findings, a number of comments on the data are relevant.

1. Census data were used in order to incorporate education and age distributions by industry and by province. Average weekly earnings were then collected to correspond to the census month of June for 1971 and 1981. Observations on earnings in retail and wholesale trade for Prince Edward Island were unavailable. This reduced the potential 60 observations to 56.

2. Data for part-time employment were found only for the 1981 census period, and these data were available only for the trade sector as a whole. Instead of dropping the use of part-time employment, a part-time variable was constructed that would reflect differences in the part-time employment rate across provinces and industries. This meant, however, that the part-time variable could be used only for 1981.

3. To capture differences in the *distribution* of ages (rather than simply the average age), the cumulative percentage of the labour force below 24 years of age was used as the measure of age. Higher values of the age variable correspond to higher percentages of the population that are less than or equal to 24 years of age.

4. The corresponding measure for the education distribution was the percentage of the labour force with education levels in high school. The frequency (rather than the cumulative) distribution was used because the percentage of the population with only elementary school education is relatively constant across industries.

Table 9
Regressions for Log (Average Weekly Earnings, in 1981 dollars)

Variable	1981		1971-81	
	Coefficient	Standard Error	Coefficient	Standard Error
Constant	7.007		6.776	
Percentage Female	−0.441	(0.491)	−0.583	(0.332)
Age	−1.420*	(0.662)	−1.662*	(0.558)
Provincial Unemployment Rate	−2.810*	(0.630)	−1.616*	(0.637)
Education	−0.866*	(0.407)	−0.546*	(0.182)
Part Time	−0.332*	(0.105)		
Retail Dummy	−0.050	(0.134)	−0.122	(0.097)
1981 Dummy			0.061	(0.070)
R^2	.908		.816	
Number of Observations	28		56	
Degrees of Freedom	21		49	

Note: * Significantly different from zero at 5 percent.

Note: The regressions using Census data were run with the regression package in Lotus. This means that the terms in brackets are standard errors rather than t-statistics.

Note: The part-time employment variable was constructed by combining three pieces of part-time information: provincial part-time employment rates, the difference in part-time employment rate across industries, and the difference across occupations. To distinguish between wholesale and retail, part-time occupation rates for sales (retail) and materials handling (wholesale) were used. The variable "part time" was constructed by multiplying the three percentages together for each grouping and then multiplying that by 1,000 (to make the units comparable with the other variables in the equation).

APPENDIX II

THE COMPARATIVE CLASS STRUCTURE PROJECT DATABASE

The Sample

Observations for all respondents who passed through certain filters were included. The self-employed were eliminated. Only those hired by the private sector were considered. Those with income from other sources were eliminated since it was not possible to identify their income from employment. The following were eliminated: those reporting no income, those who were still at school, those who did not answer the training question, those who worked 51 or more hours per week, and those who had schooling that involved night courses or correspondence (These answers were coded in a manner which was not comparable to the responses of employees with traditional schooling.). Also, individuals working in the primary sector were not considered.

The Variables

Dependent variable:

The natural logarithm of income. The income variable was reported as falling within certain bands; the mean of the class was taken as observed income and transformed into a log.

Independent Variables:

Experience: This variable was the difference between 1983 and the year that first job began.

Exp squared: Experience squared.

Apprenticeship: A dummy which was 1 if the respondent had completed an apprenticeship which was a full-time programme in a company training school lasting six weeks or more, or training in the armed forces leading to qualification in a trade; otherwise equal to 0.

Specific training: A dummy which was 1 if the respondent thought the skills used in his or her job were only applicable in the present job.

Years in school: The number of years in school altogether.

Log of hours: Natural logarithm of hours worked.

Urban: Those residing in towns or cities with more than 100,000 residents.

Commitment: The question on which the dummy was calculated was "Since you began working ...was there ever a time when you did not have a job, and did not want to find a job."

Union: A dummy which was equal to 1 if the employee belonged to a union; 0 otherwise.

Male living with wife or partner: Dummy which was 1 for respondents with both characteristics; 0 otherwise.

Construction: Dummy which was 1 if SIC code of employer was between 400 and 449.

Transportation & Communication: Dummy which was 1 if SIC code of employer was between 450 and 499.

Wholesale: Dummy which was 1 if SIC code of employer was between 500 and 599.

Retail: Dummy which was 1 if SIC code of employer was between 600 and 699.

Other services: Dummy which was 1 if SIC code of employer was between 700 and 999.

Female living alone: Dummy which was 1 for respondents with both characteristics; 0 otherwise.

Female living with husband or partner: Dummy which was 1 for respondents with both characteristics; 0 otherwise.

Prairies, B.C., Quebec, and Atlantic: Regional dummies.

Female interacting with years in school: Variable was 0 if male; equal to years of schooling if female.

Female interacting with experience: Variable was 0 if male; equal to experience if female.

The Regressions

The earnings regressions for all industries are presented in table 12 and those for the three industry groupings (wholesale, retail, and other) are presented in table 13. The "other" grouping was manufacturing, construction, transportation and communication, and other services.

Table 10
Earnings Regressions for All Industries*

Variable	Coefficient	T Value
Constant	6.89333	(20.953)
Experience	.03177	(5.611)
Experience squared	−4.14277E-04	(−3.761)
Apprenticeship	.08422	(1.560)
Specific training	−.20397	(−2.041)
Years in school	.07414	(8.036)
Log of hours	.33511	(4.320)
Urban	.16507	(3.888)
Commitment	.11477	(2.279)
Union	.12418	(2.889)
Male living with wife or partner	.24646	(3.657)
Construction	−.03839	(−.415)
Transportation and communication	.01077	(.121)
Wholesale	.03614	(.360)
Retail	−.04519	(−.549)
Other services	−.02530	(−.462)
Prairies	−4.96026E-03	(−.078)
B.C.	.09411	(1.333)
Quebec	.08684	(1.729)
Atlantic	.05736	(.714)
Female living alone	.14943	(.713)
Female living with husband or partner	.07718	(.360)
Female interacting with years in school	−4.82422E-03	(−.358)
Female interacting with experience	−5.12033E-03	(−1.488)
R^2	.42240	
Adjusted R^2	.39437	
Observations	498	

Note: * Except for primary industry.

Table 12
Earnings Regressions for Retail, Wholesale and Other Industries Grouping

Variable	Retail Coefficients (t values)	Wholesale Coefficients (t values)	Other Coefficients (t values)
Constant	8.37246	2.66850	6.91543
	(5.459)	(1.067)	(20.416)
Experience	.09433	.09850	.03013
	(3.173)	(2.182)	(2.094)
Experience squared	−1.54296E-03	−1.34474E-03	−4.05441E-04
	(−2.990)	(−1.712)	(−3.516)
Apprenticeship	.23147	−.32731	.06159
	(.945)	(−.946)	(1.060)
Specific training	−.10935	.51286	−.17256
	(−.192)	(.642)	(−1.652)
Years in school	.11758	.27932	.07148
	(2.032)	(2.264)	(7.814)
Log of hours	−.29134	.47605	.35223
	(−.897)	(.971)	(4.302)
Urban	.27687	−.01503	.13882
	(1.505)	(−.051)	(3.183)
Commitment	−.25742	.79803	.12058
	(−.994)	(1.991)	(2.312)
Union	.27146	−.20037	.13341
	(.735)	(−.580)	(3.060)
Male living with	.38061	.35470	.25555
wife or partner	(1.252)	(.930)	(3.536)
Female living alone	.58459	1.32457	.16766
	(.485)	(.755)	(.783)
Female living with	.57595	1.74482	.10463
husband or partner	(.510)	(.933)	(.474)
Female interacting	−.04242	−.02641	−7.41779E-03
with years in school	(−.524)	(−.212)	(−.536)
Female interacting	−.02571	− 07862	−4.12495E-03
with experience	(−1.501)	(−2.203)	(−1.128)
R^2	.58021	.85205	.40769
Adjusted R^2	.35417	.62190	.38785
Observations	41	24	433

Chapter 5

ORGANIZATIONAL DEVELOPMENTS

INTRODUCTION

Co-ordination and Scarcity

Without scarcity, there is no need for economizing behaviour and, *a fortiori*, no need for economic analysis. Economists analyse the implications of scarcity, and the insights derived from any economic study depend upon how scarcity is introduced into the analysis. Traditionally, economists have considered scarcity solely in relation to the limited number of goods and services that can be produced from scarce resources. In this context, the economic problem is how best to answer the social questions of "what to produce," "how to produce," and "who is to consume." However, if the analysis also assumes that the resources required to co-ordinate economic activities are not scarce, then either a social planner or a system of private markets or any other allocative alternative will be equally effective in solving these problems. In Hayek's terms:

> *If* we possess all of the relevant information, *if* we can start out from a given system of preferences, and *if* we command complete knowledge of available means, the problem is purely one of logic.[1]

When a model assumes that the co-ordination of exchange absorbs no real resources, that model cannot address the role of economic organization in lowering the costs of exchange. Although insight can be gained from the traditional literature, neither a bureaucrat in a modern government department nor a businessman in a modern corporation would recognize the absence of co-ordination problems encountered by their stylized counterparts. In the transaction costless setting, the real world problems encountered when co-ordinating economic activity are absent.

ORGANIZATIONAL ECONOMICS

Institutional Variety and Choice

When co-ordination is costly, economic agents must choose to allocate from among a variety of institutional and organizational alternatives. While the use of economic methodology to analyse these alternatives may initially seem unusual, it has proved to be both powerful and insightful in understanding the issues facing the trade sector. Moreover, the application of choice theory to organizational behaviour has been equally successful when used in either private or public settings. Thus, although political entrepreneurs and private businessmen operate in different competitive environments, both must identify what their clients will value and design the appropriate organizational mechanism for delivering it. Similarly, both the organizers and those being organized must deal with the potential divergence between promise and practice—whether or not distribution takes place through political or economic markets.

Internal Organizational Options

Any institution consists of a framework designed to encourage constructive co-ordination, either through self-enforcing agreements (i.e., ones in which it is in the self-interest of both parties to do what they have promised to do) or, where self-enforcing agreements are too expensive, through penalty and reward structures which are economical to administer and enforce.

Although it may seem counter-intuitive, the penalty structures established within organizations are often in the interest of those who might be punished by them. In the most simple example, an individual may prefer to join a club that expels members for nonpayment of dues. By subjecting oneself to the possibility of expulsion, the individual permits the club to exclude free-riders. Members choose to constrain their freedom because they are more than compensated by the increased effectiveness of the group in pursuing a common goal.[2] That the same is true in a commercial setting is illustrated vividly by the following anecdote:

> On the Yangtze River in China, there is a section of fast water over which boats are pulled upstream by a team of coolies prodded by an overseer using a whip. On one such passage an American lady, horrified at the sight of the overseer whipping the men as they strained at their harness, demanded that something be done about the brutality. She was quickly informed by the captain that nothing could be done: "These men own the right to draw boats over this stretch of water and they have hired the overseer and given him his duties."[3]

Constraints are voluntarily agreed to within an organization *if* their existence raises wealth and *if* the individuals involved receive a sufficient share of the increase to more than offset the negative effects of being constrained.

Organizational Innovation and Welfare

Organizational economists are aware that creativity can be constructive or destructive of wealth and are interested in organizational mechanisms that tilt innovation towards more constructive ends.[4] Innovations can improve our lot by reducing physical scarcity or by providing new consumption goods or by facilitating co-operation. While economists have typically focused on the first two routes, improvements in organization that permit better exploitation of our technological potential are no less important than those that increase that potential.

The realization of the potential inherent in existing technology is not a trivial problem. For a large number of reasons countries differ in their level of wealth, in the number of their homeless, and in the health of their children. Of the many reasons for these differences, access to technology is, in our opinion, a relatively minor one. Books and blueprints for blast furnace or computer technology do exist, and the experts willing to interpret them are widely available. What is much scarcer is the legal, political, and social environment that encourages and supports effective organization.

In the traditional literature of economics, retail and wholesale activities receive little attention. The problems faced by a storekeeper in transferring title, in storing commodities, in dealing with employee and customer theft, in choosing a product line, in deciding what price to charge, in weighing the pros and cons of locating in a new shopping centre, in continuing as an independent or becoming a franchise, in persuading a cynical public of his or her honesty, and in expanding regionally, nationally, or internationally are footnote material. Similarly, the problems of a customer in searching out better products, in understanding credit arrangements, and in identifying dealers who don't renege on the spirit of their warranties also receive short shrift. What is footnote material in that literature is of principal concern in our study.

In this and succeeding chapters we examine some of the organizational changes that have occurred and are occurring in the trade sector. Our policy objective is not to prescribe a blueprint for a better merchandising system but to encourage the development of a policy environment in which the individual genius of those in the public and the private sectors is channelled continuously to producing that end. An understanding of the rich mix of private and governmental institutions is a prerequisite for understanding the process creating institutional competition. This chapter focuses on the varied characteristics of the private firms in the trade sector, the strategic decisions that determine these characteristics, and the market environment in which they operate.⁵ Chapter 6 examines the role of group co-operatives and government organizations in marketing, while chapter 7 explores more complex contractual arrangements, such as franchising and shopping centres, that co-ordinate a number of independent entities to provide merchandising services.

PRIVATE BUSINESS ORGANIZATION

A Spectrum of Firms

The private sector is composed of a large number of small and medium-sized firms that coexist with a smaller number of large regional, national, and international concerns. Many of the smaller units are unincorporated single proprietorships. As table 14 indicates, just under one-third of all Canadian businesses with sales of $2 million or less were in the trade sector. In contrast, less than 6 percent of all small firms were in manufacturing.

Table 14

Distribution of Small Businesses in Canada by Industry, 1983

Industry	Number of Firms	Percent
Forestry	12,850	1.8
Mining	4,795	0.7
Manufacturing	39,910	5.6
Construction	142,848	20.0
Transportation	74,672	10.5
Trade	224,713	31.5
Real Estate	45,453	6.4
Business and Personal Services	167,684	23.5
Total	712,925	100.0

Source: Statistics Canada, 61-521.

Note: "Small" refers to firms with less than $2 million revenue.

The distribution of small businesses in the retail and wholesale sectors by size of operation as a percentage of all businesses of that scale is presented in table 15. As that table makes apparent, retail outlets dominate the smaller size classifications, while wholesale concerns are more important in the larger size classes. Considerable variation exists among the sub-

Table 15

Distribution of Small Businesses in Selected Retail and Wholesale Sectors, Canada, 1983

	Total	< $50,000	$50,000 –$99,999	$100,000 –$299,999	$250,000 –$499,999	$500,000 –$999,999	$1,000,000 –$1,999,999
Total All Industries	712,924	300,428	129,402	137,008	72,730	46,781	26,575
Wholesale	49,087	13,059	6,992	9,881	7,253	6,457	5,445
(Percent of Total)	6.9%	4.3%	5.4%	7.2%	10.0%	13.8%	20.5%
Total Retail	175,626	53,417	29,567	41,815	26,118	16,782	7,927
(Percent of Total)	24.6%	17.8%	22.8%	30.5%	35.9%	35.9%	29.8%
Clothing Stores	9,216	2,352	1,815	2,830	1,424	591	205
(Percent of Total Retail)	5.2%	4.4%	6.1%	6.8%	5.5%	3.5%	2.6%
Appliance, TV, Radio, Stereo	7,169	3,054	1,415	1,399	738	419	143
(Percent of Total Retail)	4.1%	5.7%	4.8%	3.3%	2.8%	2.5%	1.8%
Service Stations	13,592	2,857	1,323	2,271	2,730	3,065	1,345
(Percent of Total Retail)	7.7%	5.3%	4.5%	5.4%	10.5%	18.3%	17.0%
Florists	2,901	809	800	876	310	88	18
(Percent of Total Retail)	1.7%	1.5%	2.7%	2.1%	1.2%	0.5%	0.2%
Hardware	2,855	347	517	892	654	331	113
(Percent of Total Retail)	1.6%	0.6%	1.7%	2.1%	2.5%	2.0%	1.4%
Jewellery	2,872	728	653	931	370	140	49
(Percent of Total Retail)	1.6%	1.4%	2.2%	2.2%	1.4%	0.8%	0.6%

Source: Statistics Canada, 61-521.

sectors of the retail trade. Clothing stores represent 10.5 percent of the stores doing less than $100,000 in sales and only 2.6 percent of the stores with revenues between $1 and $2 million. In contrast, service stations, which provide a similar percentage (9.8) in the first category, make up 17 percent of the total retail outlets in the second.

Of the large firms in the trade sector, a few like Eaton's are private corporations but most are publicly owned. Some of Canada's largest and best-known firms, such as Weston and the Hudson's Bay Company, have the heart of their activities in the trade sector. In recent years there has been a rapid rise in the importance of chains, organizations that market their products under the same brand name and maintain uniformity among a number of different stores. The senior department stores, the junior department stores, and a growing variety of specialized stores are organized through multiple outlets. While some chains are local and some regional, a growing number of chains are organized on a national basis.

Within the trade sector, food distributors tend to be particularly large. George Weston, the Loblaw companies, Provigo, the Oshawa Group, and Steinberg's were all among the 100 most profitable companies in 1986. In that year, their return on equity varied considerably, with Provigo experiencing a rate of return above 20 percent while Steinberg's was under 7 percent. Provigo generated a profit of over $60 million, while the Oshawa Group, which had higher sales, registered a lower profit of $43 million. Steinberg's had a debt-to-equity ratio of 25 percent, which was considerably lower than that of the other four companies whose ratios were in the range of 62 to 87 percent.[6]

National estimates of the market shares of supermarkets for 1986 are presented in table 16. These shares may be misleading due to regional specialization. Data on regional shares for packaged food sales (excludes dairy and fresh produce sales) by supermarkets are presented in table 17. Firms such as Sobey's and Metro-Richelieu, which appear to have marginal importance from a national perspective, are shown to be significant players in their particular regions.

In 1986 there were no non-food wholesalers in the 100 most profitable firms in Canada. The most profitable non-food wholesaler was Finning, earning just less than $21 million. In contrast there were two large retailers, Canadian Tire and Sears Canada, in the top 100. Dylex, which owns a number of retail chains, was in the top 100 in 1985 but fell out of that category in 1986. Some of the fashion firms that rose to prominence in the retail sector in 1986 had very high rates of return on equity; examples are the Jean Coutu Group with 41 percent, Pantorama Industries with 96 percent, and Shirmax Fashions with 59 percent. At the other end of the scale, some large traditional retailers, such as the Bay and Woodward's, experienced losses.[8]

Table 16

Supermarkets—National Market Shares for 1986

Company	Sales (millions of $)	Market Share (percent)
Weston (1)	5,005	14.3
IGA	3,675	10.5
Steinberg (2)	3,605	10.3
Safeway (3)	3,220	9.2
A & P (4)	2,345	6.7
Provigo (5)	1,890	5.0
Metro-Richelieu	1,750	4.8
Sobey's (6)	595	1.6

Source: International Surveys Ltd., ISL. Table and notes are from *Financial Times*, October 26, 1987.

Notes: (1) Includes Loblaws, Real Canadian Superstore, Super Valu, Ziggy's, Zehr, Mr. Grocer and Atlantic Superstore among others.

(2) Includes Steinberg, Valdi, and Miracle Food Mart.

(3) Includes Safeway, Safeway Superstores, Food Barn and Food for Less.

(4) Includes six-month results of 93 Dominion Stores purchased April 1985.

(5) Includes Maxi and Heritage.

(6) Includes Lo Foods.

Table 17

Supermarkets—Some Regional Market Shares, 1986

(percentage market share)

	B.C.	Alberta	Saskatchewan	Manitoba	Ontario	Quebec	Maritimes
Weston	12	12	35	29	18		25–27
Safeway	26	36	19	32			
Co-Operatives		19	27				
Steinberg					13–14	20	
Provigo						22–23	
Metro-Richelieu						21	
Sobey's							24

Source: *Globe and Mail*, April 4, 1987.

ORGANIZATIONAL RESPONSES TO INFORMATIONAL AND CO-ORDINATION PROBLEMS

The Value of a Name: Building and Nurturing a Reputation for Quality

Selling offers scope for opportunistic practices. The itinerant snake oil salesman of yesteryear and the used car salesman of today face the same image problem. How can an honest retailer distinguish himself from a dishonest one? The problem is an ancient one, as illustrated by these descriptions of retailing in Toronto in the period just after Confederation.

> ... in any store it was necessary to have one's wits about oneself, for it was clearly understood that nothing was necessarily what it was purported to be. Prices on goods had no meaning; they were normally set from 40 to 60 per cent above their value to allow for bargaining. Material classed as "pure wool" might have no wool in it at all. "Imported fabrics" might have been imported from two blocks away.

> Labels meant nothing either, since well-known ones could be sewed in the shop to the shoddiest of goods. They made little impression on poor folk anyway, since few of them could read.

> Rarely were goods displayed openly; more often they were on high shelves or in glass cases. This was to foil customers who came armed with a slice of lemon to check for colour-fastness—if the touch of the acid turned the material black, it would probably run at the first washing.

> Stores were always boasting of the bargains they could offer by their shrewd purchases of "wet goods," fine imported fabrics allegedly slightly damaged by sea water *en route*. In most cases these were just unsaleable items from stock, lightly sprayed with brine from a barrel most stores kept in their basements for this purpose. (W. Stephenson, *The Store that Timothy Built*, McClelland and Stewart, 1969, pp. 15-16.)

The problem facing a wholesaler or a retailer is not simply one of recognizing that consumers value product quality and trader honesty, but rather one of convincing potential customers that promised dimensions will be delivered and customers will not be cheated. One way of assuring customers that short-term cheating possibilities will be forgone is by having sellers demonstrate that they have more to lose if their dealings with customers are not scrupulous. To do so the store owner may create a hostage or monument that is worth more than the gain from cheating.[9]

Advertising, Reputations, and Hostages

Consider, as an example, an advertising campaign by a chain of stores that promises to customers the higher level of quality products that they have been demanding. Suppose further that the advertising provides few specifics other than identifying the chain and making it obvious that the campaign is costly. In order to cover these costs, the chain must charge more than a competitor who provides the same quality but has not undertaken this advertising investment. Suppose now that the chain decides to chisel on quality but still sells output at the premium price. In this case, abnormal profits can be made as long as people are fooled. Eventually, however, customers will learn and the chain will be revealed as unreliable. The investment in advertising now becomes valueless[10] and the output becomes unsaleable except at a price consistent with its lower quality. It follows that as long as the total temporary profit that can be made from this chiselling option is less than the amount invested in the advertising campaign, it will not pay the seller to chisel. In this case, the promise of quality has credibility.[11] Image advertising (or other hostages) and the price premiums[12] for quality are two parts of a strategy designed to provide customers with information about who is honest and who is not. It survives, in many circumstances, because it is the cheapest way of dealing with a scarcity problem, the scarcity of information about who is, and who is not, an honest merchant. Being the cheapest method does not, of course, make it necessarily a cheap method.

While a social function of advertising is as a hostage or source of reliable information, the usual reliability of this signal can be used by individuals to profit from misinformation. To protect this social role and to channel competition in retail advertising towards benign paths, section 36 of the Competition Act defines a number of advertising practices as illegal. For example, firms can be prosecuted for making unsubstantiated claims for the products that they sell, for misrepresenting the normal selling price of their product, or for not having a reasonable supply of products advertised at bargain prices.

Each year the Bureau of Competition, Marketing Practices Branch, prosecutes a large number of misleading advertising and deceptive marketing practices cases. In 1985–86, over 10,000 complaints were received; complete investigations were made in about one-fifth of them; and prosecutions were begun in about 150 cases.[13] The Bureau of Competition publishes a quarterly *Misleading Advertising Bulletin* which provides details on the cases pending or just resolved. A typical case was reported as:

The accused had been convicted of two charges under section 36(1)(a) for representing that remanufactured engines had "new valves, springs, pushrods" when in fact these engine parts were not new, but reconditioned. On May 25, 1984, an appeal by the accused against conviction was dismissed, but sentence was reduced from $75,000 to $25,000 on the first charge and from $25,000 to $10,000 on the second charge, for a total fine of $35,000.[14]

The deterrent effect of these convictions would be greatly increased if more media publicity and attention were given to these cases.

Guarantees and Opportunism

Advertising is only one way of making credible a pledge to supply quality goods, and individual retailers have developed their own methods and designed combinations of existing methods depending on circumstances.[15] The key to commercial survival is to find a cheaper technique that encourages repeat business. For Timothy Eaton it was a new sales strategy—satisfaction or your money back. Like the advertising promise, the problem is credibility. A money-back guarantee is worthless if hidden in the fine print is some legal reason why the retailer is exempt from making good on the promise. Eaton's gained credibility by generally giving the customer the benefit of the doubt on returns. Such a policy is not costless, since just as there are opportunistic merchants there are opportunistic customers. In his insightful history of the Eaton company, Stephenson reports:

> One woman sent back a bed-pan she had for thirteen years, explaining it was the wrong shape. She got her refund.

and

> What many Eatonians consider the ultimate in some sort of gall, however, involved a man, not a woman—a *clergyman* at that. He brought back for refund a suit he'd worn for three years, with the explanation that he'd just noticed it was dark brown, not *black* as he'd ordered.[16]

The art in retailing is to build a reputation for delivering value for money. Once developed, however, that reputation has public goods characteristics that can be exploited commercially by expanding those activities positively influenced by the reputation. At least some of the contractions and expansions, changes in merchandise mix, and shifts in ownership relations can be explained as attempts to take commercial advantage of economies associated with brand and reputational capital.

Capitalizing on a Reputation for Quality and Value

One of the earliest ways of using the scale possibilities of reputational capital was through a chain of similar stores. Capitalizing on brand name, however, requires a configuration of store types consistent with the productivity of that capital. A national distribution network, for example, is feasible for a chain that markets high-volume, middle-quality merchandise to broad population groupings. However, for a chain specializing in high-quality goods aimed at a sub-group of the high-income population, coverage must be limited to a few stores in the larger cities. Table 18 illustrates the point with the store distribution of three chains from the Dylex group. Fairweather and Tip Top Tailors are of the first type; Harry Rosen is of the second.

Table 18
Regional Distribution of Stores for Three Chains in 1983

	Fairweather	Tip Top Tailors	Harry Rosen
B.C.	15	35	1
Alberta	18	42	1
Saskatchewan	3	10	0
Manitoba	5	13	0
Ontario	58	128	10
Quebec	7	31	1
New Brunswick	5	11	0
Nova Scotia	7	5	0
Newfoundland	2	6	0

Source: Dylex Annual Report 1983.

The Harry Rosen chain, which began selling men's clothing in 1961, attempted to take advantage of its reputation for quality by moving into women's clothing in 1981. Whether a reputation will be transferable to new stores, new product lines, and a new clientele is difficult to judge, but in this case the early results are favourable. As early as 1983, the Harry Rosen women's stores were among those generating the highest dollar value of sales per square foot of the Dylex chains.[17]

With an increasingly mobile population, knowledge of local reputations for quality is no longer necessary for a traveller outside his or her home territory. Part of the brand capital of national and regional chains is the reputation for maintaining *uniformity* in the quality of service and product promised in their different outlets. These chains can thereby cater to a traveller's demand for predictability in the quality of his or her purchases.

Cross-Merchandising and Concentration

Exploiting reputations for quality is not the only reason firms alter structure or focus. Businesses in the trade sector also adjust the span of their activities to profit from changes arising in personnel mix, new technology, new perceptions of how to save the shopper time, or accumulated experience. Building centres begin to supply tools complementary to building products and thus enter the traditional merchandising area of hardware stores. Drugstores expand into "department store type merchandise" (DSTM), while food stores expand the shelf space dedicated to cosmetics and non-prescription medicines. Clothing stores that cater to a wealthy clientele, such as Creed's or Holt Renfrew, gain experience with their consumers' tastes and add complementary accessories and gourmet foods. There is now so much commingling of product types that in the Regional Municipality of Ottawa-Carleton (RMOC), where the authors live, the department store share of DSTM was estimated at only 38 percent in 1985.[18]

Table 19 summarizes the market shares of Canadian department stores in 1986. These figures tend to overstate national concentration levels because of the extensive sales of DSTM through other retail categories. On the other hand, cross-ownership of legally separate chains tends to act in the opposite direction (e.g., the Bay, Zellers, and Simpsons are part of the same ownership complex).

Table 19
Department Stores—National Market Ratios, 1986

Company	Sales (millions of $)	Market Share (percent)
Sears Canada(1)	2,603	20.4
Eaton's	1,841	14.5
The Bay(2)	1,765	13.9
Zellers	1,731	13.6
Woolco	1,587	12.5
K Mart	1,143	9.0
Woodwards(3)	724	5.7
Simpsons(2)	644	5.1
Towers-Bonimart	444	3.5

Source: Based on information from industry sources. Table and notes are from *Financial Times*, October 26, 1987.

Notes: (1) Excludes catalogue sales.
      (2) Accounts for eight Simpsons stores transferred to the Bay in August 1986.
      (3) Excludes food sales.

Like the case of supermarket retailing discussed above, low national concentration ratios can mask much higher concentration levels in distinct regional and local markets. However, even if this is the case, high concentration ratios will not reflect market power if entry barriers are relatively low. By and large, retail markets are highly contestable, particularly because much of the organizational and physical capital, such as inventories, is not sunk and can be shifted across different markets whenever high profits signal market opportunities. Entry costs are also low because existing stores in competing industries can easily shift their product portfolios. As we have seen above, the supply of DSTM is highly elastic because a variety of store types other than department stores can readily add some subset of DSTM to their existing offerings.

Despite these considerations, competition authorities have shown concern whenever mergers threaten to raise concentration. The takeover of the food operations of the Woodward's department store chain by Canada Safeway provides a recent example. This merger would have increased market concentration in 17 urban markets in British Columbia and Alberta. In May 1987, the Director of Investigation and Research announced that he would apply to have the new Competition Tribunal review the proposed acquisition. After negotiation, the Director withdrew his application when Canada Safeway agreed: (a) to divest its interests in 12 of the retail stores in 6 of the affected markets; (b) to run the acquired stores independently of Safeway's other food retailing operations; (c) not to identify the stores as Safeway stores; and (d) to maintain home delivery and other traditional Woodward's services.[19]

The Woodward's case illustrates one instance where cross-merchandising within a single firm was revealed to be less profitable than cross-merchandising between two different firms operating in the same physical locations. Historically, food distribution has been a marginal offering of the department stores, with some firms divesting and others expanding into that activity as their general profitability has fluctuated. At the moment, the Woodward's chain is in a period of retrenchment.

In the gasoline sector, both the independents and the integrated oil companies have experimented with offering car washes and assorted merchandise at their outlets. Generally the oil companies have not been successful at cross-merchandising, but the combination of a convenience store with gasoline sales has brought success to the Perrette Dairy Ltd. chain and has been imitated more recently by larger chains of convenience stores.

One reason the combination of a convenience store and gasoline outlet has been successful in Quebec is because it "is not required by law that a clerk be dedicated to the sale of gasoline; the store and the gas bar can share the labor costs."[20]

Cross-Ownership of Chains

Successful management in one chain sometimes leads to more complex structures. For example, a number of food distribution chains have begun to develop chains in other retailing areas. The Oshawa Group, a food wholesaler which supplies 474 franchised IGA outlets and 105 corporately run food stores, also owns 72 drugstores and a number of department stores. Similarly, in 1984 Canada Safeway opened 10 pharmacies in Alberta and Manitoba and increased this number to 34 in the following year.

Specialized national chains usually have evolved from a successful single store or local chain. Continued success has led to the evolution of specialists in running and managing a portfolio of chains. Dylex, for example, owns and operates a number of clothing store chains in addition to those appearing in table 17. Among these are Town & Country, B.H. Emporium, Braemar, Suzy Shier, Rubys/Feathers, Harry Rosen Women, and Big Steel Man.

One of the co-founders of Dylex, William Posluns, revealed in an interview the type of organizational strategy behind their success.[21] Dylex encourages its managers to own shares in the company and gives the top management of its chains extensive leeway to make their own decisions. One example of the complex arrangements that are made to provide the appropriate incentives to talented retailers in large organizations concerned Harry Rosen. Mr. Rosen sold his stores to Dylex in the late sixties to become the manager of the then troubled Tip Top chain. Tip Top stores became profitable under his leadership but the Rosen stores began to lose money. Rosen then agreed to buy back a 49 percent interest in the Harry Rosen chain and return as its manager.

Variations in Store Types and Sizes: Responses to Growing Specialization in Demand

Accompanying the search for new product lines that cross traditional merchandising boundaries is a competitive process of consolidation and specialization within store types. Even as the range of food outlets has widened with the introduction of new megastores of over 70,000 square feet, there has been the dramatic growth of a dazzling array of small bakeries, delicatessens, natural food outlets, and ethnic and other specialized stores. Retail entrepreneurs compete to respond to the changing demands that have resulted from urbanization, multiculturalism, higher incomes, and increasing numbers of working couples. In turn, the chains study demographic patterns and trends at home and abroad before targeting a store at a new segment of the market. As an illustration, Dylex introduced the B.H. Emporium chain to sell to the female teenage market, and Zellers opened its Just Kids stores in 1983 to specialize in children's wear. At the other extreme, the growing disposable income of senior citizens has resulted in marketing campaigns targeting this group. For instance, Eaton's, Shoppers Drug Mart, and various movie theatres periodically offer discounts to senior citizens. In Toronto, a clothing store, Emma Burton Fashions, featuring clothes suitable to women over 50, has recently opened.[22]

Retailers also experiment with new alignments of products and partitions of their space. One such development is the store-within-a-store concept. The department stores create a number of boutiques within their stores to carry competing private brands, and supermarkets establish self-contained units as internal delis, cheese shops, and wine departments. Senior Canadian department stores have also expanded into the marketing (and in some cases the provision) of professional and financial services. Sears Canada owns 25 percent of Allstate Insurance Co. of Canada,[23] which has outlets in most Sears department stores. With greater financial deregulation occurring in Canada, the marketing efforts in this direction will become more pronounced.

Stylized Life Cycle of a Store

The life cycle of a store type has the following stylized elements. Once a store type becomes defined in the industry, imitative entry occurs, stimulating intense competition. This is followed by a period of consolidation among the surviving stores. Relatively slow growth then ensues, and a rise in the size of the representative store often accompanies a decline in the market share of the store type. The phenomenon of the rising size of outlets in mature retail sectors can be observed in a number of areas. Between 1966 and 1976, the sales of senior department stores declined by only 19 percent as the number of outlets fell by 36 percent.[24] In the traditional food chains, the square footage of newly opened stores has been steadily growing.[25] In this case, increased sales are sustained by fewer but bigger outlets.

A similar trend has been evident in gasoline marketing. Gasoline is sold by independents, by the franchisees of regional and national oil companies, and by the outlets directly owned by those firms. In the decade between 1974 and 1984, independents held about 15 percent of the market. This percentage varies by region and has usually been highest in Ontario and lowest in the Atlantic region. The independents have had less success in the Maritimes in part because Irving Oil, which was an independent, became the region's largest refiner and refused to sell to independents. Regulatory constraints imposed in Nova Scotia and in Prince Edward Island also make it more difficult for independents to become established.[26]

Integrated oil companies often market their product under a number of brands. These no-frills offerings, designed to contest the offerings of the independents, have been called, somewhat picturesquely, fighting brands. For example, Suncor's second brands, Pronto and Baron, represented 13 percent of total sales in 1982.[27] Many of these fighting brands have been removed from the market, presumably because their win-loss records were disappointing.

The rise in size of the average outlet and the reduction in number of outlets in gasoline marketing has been remarkable. Between 1970 and 1980, the number of outlets in the industry decreased by 11,751 while the average volume per outlet increased from 130,000 gallons per year to 319,000. The increase in volume was concentrated in urban self-serve outlets. Because the self-service station provides essentially one product and not the same flexible range of outputs as a full-service station, the control problems that have inhibited many chains are less pronounced. As a result, these stations have tended to remain company-owned outlets, rather than become franchises. As organizational issues would suggest, sales from company-owned outlets have increased dramatically. In this regard, Imperial Oil is typical of the industry. Company-controlled sales as a percentage of total sales rose from 7 percent in 1970 to 47 percent in 1980.[28]

Strategic Planning and Competition

Finding the right strategy and integrating new technologies into an organization is one key to success in retailing. When Timothy Eaton opened his retail outlet in Toronto shortly after Confederation, he combined his offer of a money-back guarantee with the sale of goods for cash only and at fixed prices. The more usual selling practices of that day are reflected in the following description:

> Even small establishments often had four or five clerks, for a single sale might take all day to transact, allowing for bargaining on both sides. There was no question of delivery on most portable items, because wary patrons didn't trust any store to deliver the same goods they had purchased. Substitution of poorer merchandise was easy, and the buyer had no redress.[29]

The same account describes how ubiquitous barter was in contrast to payment in cash:

> There were few fixed prices in these country stores. A pound of butter, the end product of hours of churning by wife or children, might be extended for a plug of Cavendish Twist tobacco or say 10 to 12 cents in "store

credits." A barrel of salt pork or several bushels of grain might be worth a bolt of gingham, a gallon of whisky, several dollars in credits—or *all* of these, depending on how good a haggler the vendor was.[30]

Eaton's early sales strategies were immensely successful, but initial success did not prevent it from changing its strategies. In the changed circumstances following the Second World War, Eaton's found it profitable to revert to the practice of allowing credit sales. Innovations are risky and the return on successful efforts must more than make up for those that are not. Certainly some initiatives at Eaton's proved to be mistakes. In 1912, for example, Eaton's experimented with selling automobiles but was not successful.[31] Sometimes good ideas are developed at the wrong time. Eaton's introduced groceterias into their department stores, an innovation that could be "regarded as the first self-service supermarket chain in Canada."[32] Although this food distribution system fared better in some regions than in others, it was before its time and was withdrawn as a general feature of an Eaton's department store.

Sometimes the failure of an organizational type is by omission, a failure to adapt to changing circumstances. All the senior department stores in Canada languished in the late fifties and early sixties, as the suburbs expanded and the downtown areas contracted. The junior department stores were quicker to respond to this geographic shift of purchasing power. Only in 1964 did Eaton's and Simpsons combine to anchor the Yorkdale Shopping Centre. In subsequent years, the regional mall formula permitted the senior department stores to recapture some lost ground.[33]

Pricing Strategies and Retail Price Maintenance

Adaptation to a new environment may involve new pricing strategies. For instance, a manufacturer may wish to control the price charged at the retail level. It is sometimes thought that the only reason for maintaining a particular retail price would be as part of a conspiracy among manufacturers to raise the price at the manufacturing level.[34] For this reason, retail price maintenance was made illegal under section 38 of the Competition Act. However, manufacturers may have efficiency reasons for controlling retail prices. By requiring a higher sales margin, but forbidding price competition, manufacturers can focus retail competition on the provision of better information services to customers. If discount houses can offer the product at a lower price (by not providing the service), some customers will obtain information at the high-price store and buy at the low-price one. The high-price store may fail so that in the new equilibrium no reliable information services are made available to consumers. Variants of this argument stress unpriced outputs or the superiority of the spatial or temporal coverage of retailing if the manufacturer has the ability to control the retail price.[35] If it were costless to determine what the true story was, retail price maintenance would be legal as long as it was efficient. A prohibition is justified if the cost of making that determination is too high and the expected damage from cartel pricing exceeds the expected efficiency benefit.

Each year a few retail price maintenance cases are prosecuted. A typical example, reported in the annual report of the Director of Investigation and Research for 1986, concerned a jeweller who launched a complaint in 1981. In his complaint the jeweller charged that he had been refused supply by the Bulova Watch Company Limited because of his policy of selling at low prices. At the end of 1985 the accused pleaded guilty and was fined $10,000.[36]

Mail Order, Then and Now

Once a system exists that identifies a group of individuals and offers favorable terms on goods that appeal to them, a retailing organization will then look for new ways of marketing those products. During the late nineteenth century, Montgomery Ward and Sears initiated mail-order selling to serve on a large scale the rural and small-town population of the United States.[37] In both these cases, the firms developed a mail-order business first, and only later did they expand into selling through stores. As late as 1925, Sears relied on its mail-order business, beginning only then to turn to the task of building a retail store network.[38] In contrast, Eaton's pioneered mail-order techniques in 1884 by grafting them onto its successful store retailing system.[39] With the decline of the rural population, the catalogue business became marginal for the senior department stores in Canada. Only Sears is still active in the field.

In the United States, an active, urban-oriented direct-mail retail system has sprung up as the contemporary counterpart to the department store mail-order service. Hundreds of stores print and distribute catalogues that vary in their coverage from specialized to even more narrowly specialized. In 1986, *The New Yorker* magazine ran an advertising section where "prestigious mail- and phone-order companies" were invited to inform readers about their catalogues. The reader was told the line of specialization and the price of the catalogue. Ninety-nine companies paid to be included. Twenty-two of these catalogues were free; the price of the others clustered around $2, but some were more expensive. For example, for $25 AMG would send a catalogue answering the retail needs of a select subset of the population:

> Make your Mercedes more equal than all the rest with our exclusive Mercedes-only catalogue. Sophisticated interior appointments, scintillating Euro-look exteriors, soul-stirring performance enhancements, more.[40]

The Gucci autumn/winter catalogue and Gucci timepieces had separate entries. Patagonia offered clothes for "crossing the Kihitna Pass, racing off Cape Flattery...." Young urban professionals were invited to shop everywhere from the Banana Republic to Gump's without leaving their living rooms. Many have replied positively to such invitations.

Canadian specialized stores, such as Tilley's, have also developed a phone and mail business, but the profit potential is less because of the smaller size of the Canadian market.[41] A free trade agreement would change that. With a single market, local merchants would face increased competition from American catalogue sellers, but Canadian manufacturers and merchants would also have the opportunity to sell through this mechanism on a North American basis. For many small, quality-oriented specialty stores in Canada's poorer regions, there will be an opportunity that has never existed before. What L.L. Bean can do from Maine, some enterprising Maritimer should be able to surpass.

National and International Expansion

As some chains expand into new regions of the country or across borders,[42] others contract. A retailing formula that succeeds in one region or country is not guaranteed success in another. In some cases expansion fails because of the financial complexities encountered. The lower profits for the Dylex group in 1986 and 1987, for example, were widely attributed to difficulties in absorbing its American investment in BR Investors Inc., operators of three retailing chains including the 800-store Brooks chain. New management has been brought in and stores that previously catered to the young teenager and under-35 woman were more narrowly focused on co-ordinated sportswear for young women.[43] Another successful Canadian retailer, Canadian Tire, lost heavily in its attempt to export its retailing formula to the United States through its White Stores, Inc. subsidiary. Regional expansion has also had its casualties. Safeway's Canadian subsidiary has been very successful in Western Canada, but expansion into Toronto was discontinued in 1985. Safeway of Canada has found Germany to be friendlier territory than Toronto; it successfully operates 25 stores in West Germany.

A common method of expansion for Canadian firms has been by taking over existing chains. Shortly after the Second World War, Loblaws expanded its American holdings dramatically by acquiring an American chain, National Tea. In 1986, the American food sales of Weston (which includes the National Tea results) were over $2.7 billion, but earnings per dollar of sales were smaller in the United States than in Canada. The most recent notable example is the takeover of Allied Corp. and Federated

Department Stores Inc. in the U.S. by Canadian entrepreneur Robert Campeau.

To illustrate the constant realignment of structures that must take place to maintain competitiveness, it is instructive to look at the changes that have been initiated by Campeau.[44] Before the takeover, Allied had 24 operating divisions; after the takeover, Campeau announced plans to sell 16 of them. Of these, 11 were sold quickly for 900 million dollars. Because of the need for cash to finance the Federated takeover, Brooks Brothers, which Campeau had originally intended to keep, was sold to the British firm, Marks & Spencer for $770 million dollars (U.S.) and the Ann Taylor chain was added to those on the block. Macy's who were the main rival for Federated abandoned the pursuit when they were offered the right to buy Bullocks-Bullocks Wilshire and I. Magnin for 1.1 billion dollars (U.S.). Currently, Campeau Corp.'s debt is 3.68 million dollars and some analysts are concerned about its ability to weather a recession in retail sales. Nevertheless, except for the national department stores, the largest retailer in the United States currently is a Canadian

A regional example of expansion by takeover is the planned acquisition of D.H. Howden of London, Ontario, by Sodisco Inc. of Victoriaville, Quebec (a large wholesaler of plumbing, hardware, and building supplies). Howden is a national distributor of such products. Unlike the Campeau takeover of Allied, the fit between the two companies requires no major shift in strategy for either partner. The acquired company will "continue as a separate company and management will remain unchanged."[45] The combined sales will be over $300 million.

The internationalization of ownership in retailing is a growing phenomenon. In 1979 at least 11 percent of total grocery store sales in the U.S. took place through foreign-owned outlets. The most marked trend in ownership has been the takeover of American companies by European ones, beginning in earnest in the 1970s. Such American institutions as Saks and Marshall Fields are now foreign-owned. Grand Union was taken over by a British firm; Fed Mart became part of Mann GmbH (German); Dillard and Outlet Stores was acquired by Vroom & Dreesmann (Dutch); A&P became German-owned; Korvettes was sold to the French firm Agache Willot.[46]

Changes of ownership have provided the stimulation to realign the new acquisitions to fit the experiences and retailing strategies of the new ownership. For example, A&P had over 1,800 stores when taken over in 1979. Its new owners, the Tengelmann Group, closed about 130 stores and invested over $100 million. Some new techniques, such as box marketing, which had been successful in Germany, were introduced without much success, and the new parent found it difficult to realize the expectations it held when it bought the venerable American chain.[47]

The foreign presence in Canadian wholesaling and retailing is significant but much less than in manufacturing. In 1984, Canadian-controlled corporations accounted for just over 81 percent of sales, owned 82 percent of the assets, and earned an even larger percentage, 86.1, of profits in the trade sector.[48] Foreign ownership is more important among the large firms in the industry. Of the 347 firms in the trade sector with assets in excess of $25 million, 141 were foreign-controlled.[49]

Because of the physical proximity, the cultural overlap resulting in unexploited brand name capital, and language similarities in two-thirds of the country, American firms have naturally considered Canada when developing expansion plans. Woolworth's led the junior department stores by moving into Canada as early as 1907. In the senior department store category, Sears came into Canada in a joint venture with Simpsons in 1953.[50] It operates over 70 department stores, concentrated in suburban sites, four catalogue distribution centres, and over 1,200 catalogue sales offices in Canada. With the internationalization of the trade sector, formerly American subsidiaries have become European subsidiaries. Also, European chains such as Boots and Marks and Spencer have staked a claim in the Canadian market.

In the recent past, expansion into Canada by acquisition required a foreign buyer to gain the approval of the Foreign Investment Review Agency or its successor, Investment Canada. Marks and Spencer, for example, was permitted to acquire Peoples Department Stores Ltd. in 1975 after agreeing, *inter alia,* to open 14 new stores creating 550 new jobs, and to expand its purchasing in Canada.[51] After experiencing difficulties in the Canadian market, these terms were renegotiated in 1977.[52] The 1985 takeover of Classic Bookshops by W.H. Smith Canada Ltd. was accompanied by a commitment:

> that once Classic has established a track record of profitability, expected within three to five years, Smith will make a public offering in Canada of an additional number of shares which will make it possible for Canadians to own 49 percent of the new merged company.[53]

The Span of Business Across Sectors

Large retailers, wholesalers, and manufacturers are always calculating whether there are gains from vertical integration. As early as 1892, after consolidating its position in the retail sector, the T. Eaton Co. Ltd. expanded into wholesaling by incorporating Wilson & Co. Large retailers have both contracted to have private brands produced for them by manufacturers and expanded into manufacturing these products themselves. Weston produces a wide array of bakery and food products that it markets both to its own retail companies and to non-related companies. Dylex produces clothes for its retail outlets through a number of consolidated and unconsolidated companies.

The marketing of private labels by the large retail chains appears to be on the increase, particularly by food stores. There are very few product groupings in Loblaws that do not have a President's Choice or a No Name version. The relative credibility of the store's brand name versus the product's brand name appears to be shifting. In the west, Safeway produces its own produce through its Empress and Lucerne divisions. In 1982, it sold more than $14 million worth of food products from Canadian processors to affiliated stores in the United States and to overseas distributors.[54]

The history of any large retailer is marked by ebbs and flows into and out of the manufacture of some of the products it sells. One advantage to the retailer is more direct control over quality, and another is possibly cheaper adjustment of ordering and inventory policy. However, much of what can be achieved by vertical integration can be obtained through complex supply contracts with manufacturers. These contracts allow the retailer to avoid the managerial costs of controlling a totally different type of operation.

On occasion, manufacturers have diversified into and out of retailing as portfolio investments rather than investments that enhanced the efficient marketing of products they produced. For example, Molson Companies Ltd. recently announced plans to sell its Quebec retail hardware and building materials business (Beaver Lumber) to Groupe Val Royal Inc. for $10.7 million. Val Royal operates nine outlets in wholesale and retail plumbing, hardware, and building materials in the Greater Montreal area. The acquisition will more than double the volume of Val Royal's business.[55]

In other instances, manufacturers seek control over the retailing function to ensure that quality is not dissipated by the retailer and to influence the geographic dispersion of the stores retailing their products. Another motivation is to capture more of the brand value created by the quality control and advertising of the manufacturer. Some manufacturers, like Ralph Lauren, have begun by marketing through independent stores and developed their own outlets after accumulating a reputation.

In this chapter a picture of the retail and wholesale sectors has been painted which emphasizes the ebb and flow of institutional change, of innovation and adaptation. A process exists that encourages purposeful variety. The emphasis here has been on the private sector which dominates the distributive trades. In the next chapter, the less important but still significant role played by co-operatives and government in retailing and wholesaling is examined.

NOTES

1. F.A. Hayek, "The Use of Knowledge in Society," *American Economic Review*, 35, No.4 (September 1945), 519. While Hayek's analysis focused on the information services required to plan economic activity across two organizational alternatives, his point is easily generalizable to all organizational forms.

2. A number of socially condoned seemingly coercive acts are really *ex ante* voluntary constraints. For example, the practice in many cultures of making brothers responsible for their brothers' widows can be understood as a family organized and enforced insurance scheme.

3. Story attributed to Steven Cheung; appears in John McManus, "The Costs of Alternative Economic Organizations," *Canadian Journal of Economics*, VIII, no. 3, (August 1975) n. 3.

4. That is, organizational changes may arise to redistribute existing economic rents rather than to create new rents. Such innovations lead to the dissipation of economic rents.

5. Readers interested in the evolution of retailing in Canada will find more numbers in Statistics Canada, *Trends in Canadian Marketing*. It provides historical data on retailing up to 1964.

6. Figures are from *Report on Business Magazine, 1000 Ranking Corporate Performance in Canada* (July 1987).

7. Canadian Tire retails largely through franchised outlets.

8. Data are from *Report on Business Magazine, 1000 Ranking Corporate Performance in Canada* (July 1987), in particular the section on profitability (pp. 101-130), and on retail and wholesale (pp. 75-76). If the company was not sufficiently profitable during the year to be listed in that publication, data are from its annual report.

9. Cf. B. Klein and K. Leffler, "Non-Governmental Enforcement of Contracts: The Role of Market Forces in Assuring Quality," *Journal of Political Economy*, v. 87, no. 6 (December 1979), and O. Williamson, "Credible Commitments: Using Hostages to Support Exchange," *American Economic Review*, 83 (September 1983).

10. The advertising that promised higher quality now has negative value to the cheater since it increases customers' awareness of the forgone trading possibilities.

11. Note that while the size of the monument will depend upon the gains that can be made in the short run by cheating, this solution becomes viable when the cost of establishing reputation (value of cheating) is exceeded by the willingness of consumers to pay for higher quality.

12. This is a premium above the added cost of manufacturing and storing the better quality of good.

13. Director of Investigation and Research, Consumer and Corporate Affairs, *Annual Report for the year ended March 31, 1986*, p. 87.

14. Bureau of Competition Policy, Consumer and Corporate Affairs, *Misleading Advertising Bulletin* (April/June, 1987) p. 6.

15. The imposing structures of the older downtown branches of Canadian banks are more visible examples of how the banks solved their reputation problem. The less permanent structure of the newer suburban bank branch has become possible because of the organizational innovation of deposit insurance. With deposit insurance, the surety of the customer's deposit no longer depends upon the reliability of the bank.

16. W. Stephenson, *The Store that Timothy Built* (McClelland and Stewart 1969) p. 89 and p. 254, respectively.

17. Dylex Annual Report 1983, p. 3.

18. Larry Smith and Associates, *Retail Facilities in the RMOC* (Study prepared for the Regional Municipality of Ottawa-Carleton, June 17, 1985).

19. Information on the case is available in Backgrounder releases by the Department of Consumer and Corporate Affairs. A useful summary appears in *Canadian Competition Policy Record*, vol. 8, no. 2 (June 1987) p. 7.

20. Restrictive Trade Practices Commission, *Competition in the Canadian Petroleum Industry* (Ottawa, 1986) p. 317.

21. *Globe and Mail*, June 11, 1987.

22. *Report on Business Magazine* (July, 1987) p. 76.

23. Sears *Annual Report* 1985.

24. Statistics Canada, *Department Stores in Canada 1923-1976* (Ottawa, March 1979).

25. For example, the new store openings reported by Canada Safeway in its annual reports for 1978 to 1981 were 33,200, 37,850, 38,850, and 40,000 square feet respectively. The figure hasn't been reported in subsequent annual reports, but the four megastores opened in Edmonton and Calgary in 1984 were over 68,000 square feet in size.

26. Restrictive Trade Practices Commission, *Competition in the Canadian Petroleum Industry* (Ottawa, 1986) p. 302.

27. Ibid, p. 307.

28. Ibid, p. 315.

29. W. Stephenson, *The Store that Timothy Built* (McClelland and Stewart 1969) pp. 15-16.

30. Ibid, p. 13.

31. Ibid, p. 71.

32. Ibid, p. 87.

33. A history of department stores in Canada is provided in Statistics Canada, *Department Stores in Canada 1923 - 1976* (Ottawa 1979).

34. It has sometimes been contended that retail price maintenance has been introduced by the manufacturers in order to permit monopoly power to be exercised at the retail level. The distributors "buy" the manufacturers to do so by offering a higher price to them. If the distribution side is a tight cartel, it is not clear why they would need such a convoluted "contract" to achieve their purposes, or why they would want to share the pot with the manufacturers.

35. Cf. G.F. Mathewson and R.A. Winter, "Vertical Integration by Contractual Restraints in Spatial Markets" *Journal of Business* 56, no. 4 (1983), "An Economic Theory of Vertical Restraints," *Rand Journal of Economics* 15, no. 1 (1984), "The Economics of Vertical Restraints in Distribution," in *New Developments in the Analysis of Market Structures,* J. Stiglitz and F. Mathewson (eds.) (MIT Press, 1986). An excellent appraisal of the issue is given by R. D. Anderson and S.D. Khosla, "Recent Developments in the Competition Policy Treatment of Resale Price Maintenance," *Canadian Competition Policy Record,* v. 6, no. 4 (December 1986).

36. Director of Investigation and Research, Consumer and Corporate Affairs Canada, *Annual Report for the Year Ended March 31, 1986* p. 59.

37. A.D. Chandler, *Strategy and Structure: Chapters in the History of the American Industrial Enterprise* (MIT Press 1962) ch. 5.

38. Once committed, the company moved very quickly, and had 246 stores opened by 1928. Ibid, p. 235.

39. Eaton's maintained a different purchasing organization for mail-order business. When Sears in the United States planned to move into store retailing, it ordered a study of the Eaton's system, but rejected it in favour of a unified system. Chandler, ibid., p. 239.

40. *The New Yorker*, September 1, 1986, p.65.

41. Tilley's has circumvented this problem by servicing American customers for its hat from an American address. The wider the spectrum of products the less viable is this alternative to a Canadian retailer. For some outlets that concentrate on merchandise suitable for gifts, the tariff is less important, since in Canada and many other countries, a gift addressed to a third party can enter duty free (as long as its value is less than some threshold amount).

42. Expansion abroad is not a new phenomenon. Loblaws first entered the American market in 1939. However, the frequency of international and regional realignments has substantially increased.

43. Cf. story in *Globe and Mail*, June 11, 1987. Even this restructuring was unsuccessful, and Dylex has recently written off its investment in Brooks.

44. At the time of a takeover, realignment is also spurred by the exigencies of financing the acquisition.

45. *Globe and Mail*, May 16, 1987.

46. M.P. Kacker, *Transatlantic Trends in Retailing* (Quorum 1985) p. xiii.

47. Cf. Kacker, p. 77.

48. Statistics Canada, *Annual Report of the Minister of Supply and Services Canada under the Corporations and Labour Unions Returns Act 1984* (Statistics Canada, 1987) p. 64.

49. Ibid, p. 65.

50. The Hudson's Bay Co. acquired Simpsons in 1979 and with it a 35.6 percent interest in Simpsons-Sears. In 1983, it sold 17.6 million class B shares to Sears Roebuck and Co. at $12 per share.

51. Foreign Investment Review Agency, *News Release* (June 17, 1975).

52. F. Swedlove, "Foreign Investment in the Service Sector," *Foreign Investment Review* (Autumn 1980).

53. Investment Canada, *Communique* (Sept. 26, 1985).

54. Annual report.

55. *Globe and Mail,* May 16, 1987.

Chapter 6

CO-OPERATIVES AND
GOVERNMENT MARKETING

INTRODUCTION

Although private firms are dominant in the trade sector, co-operatives and government retailers are important in certain regions and for certain products. The main differences between co-operatives and commercial enterprises are the decision-making procedures and the motivation for making decisions.

In Canada, government wholesaling and retailing are important only in alcohol and in petroleum products. We have limited our discussion to alcohol sales. In this instance, government sellers are frequently in a monopoly position. The government board makes decisions and residual income accrues to the Treasury. Constraints are provided not by trade competitors but by political competition.

CO-OPERATIVES

Decision-Making and Financing

Corporations are controlled by the owners of the shares. An owner of 10,000 shares counts as much as 100 owners of 100 shares each. For a co-op, each member has one vote, and there is no direct way in which differences in the intensity of interest in the outcome can be registered. Co-operatives do issue shares to members for purposes of raising capital and these may be held in different amounts by each member. A "dividend," which is prescribed in the co-operative's bylaws and which must be less than a statutory ceiling, is paid on each class of shares. Another form of dividend, a "patronage dividend," can be paid to members based on their purchases during the year. In a co-op the mechanisms for rewarding decision-makers for initiatives designed to increase efficiency are less well developed than in a firm, where owners and managers have a clear motivation to take measures that increase profits. It follows that co-ops should, on average, incur higher costs, be less innovative, but also be less prone to indulge in sharp practices than firms.[1]

The Co-operative Structure

Co-operatives are a pervasive organizational form in Canada. They are a dominant form in grain marketing and a rapidly growing one in finance; in wholesale and retail, co-operatives are important but, outside the marketing of farm produce, their relative share has been declining. Most co-operatives are organized at a local level. These local co-ops in turn "own" the provincial or regional co-operatives which serve their needs. In English Canada, many of these provincial and regional institutions belong to a national association, the Co-operative Union of Canada, while the Conseil Canadien de la Co-opération plays a similar role for 2,500 co-operatives with French-speaking members. Over 300 of these are located outside the province of Quebec. These third-tier organizations provide lobbying and community relations services for the co-operative movement, as well as international development services.

Local co-operatives are typically organized under provincial law.[2] Co-operative decision-making is reflected in the constitutional right of members to air their concerns. Most members receive a positive feeling from participation, but to some, the participation factor will be a negative factor (or avoided) because of the time cost involved. Commercial retailers have complained that they are disadvantaged in competition with the co-ops because the co-ops do not pay corporate taxes.

Co-operatives in the Trade Sector

Predictably, co-operatives in retail are more successful in small towns and rural communities where members know each other and shopping is a social event and where the pace of life puts less pressure on the resident's time. Retail co-operatives have done well in the West, Quebec, and Atlantic Canada, and poorly in Ontario. One source estimates that $3.8 billion of sales were made in 1986 from Canadian retail co-operatives.[3] Many of the units are small, but the Calgary Co-operative Association Limited, for example, has 14 locations, 260,000 member-customers, and annual sales of over $370 million.[4]

Traditionally, co-operatives were viewed as a particularly attractive alternative when customers faced a monopoly local seller. An interesting historical illustration is the establishment of the Sydney Co-operative Society Ltd. in Nova Scotia in 1903, following a suggestion by MacKenzie King, who had gone there as Minister of Labour to help settle a strike. King later recalled the incident in giving testimony to the 1907 Parliamentary Committee studying a proposed Co-operative Act:

> I made a suggestion to them—to the company and to the men—that the difficulty might in part be met were an effort made in a co-operative direction; the company assisting them in getting coal at a reduced rate, the men starting a store whereby they could purchase necessities themselves, and instead of all the profits going to the dealers, they would be able to make a small saving on their purchases. The department sent them some books on co-operation and Mr. Wherry has written me that the society has been doing good work, although on a limited scale, and has really been the means of helping the working men to appreciate the difficulties of the capitalist, as well as a means of enabling them to meet some of the difficulties with which they had to contend themselves.[5]

Like the Sydney store, most of the co-ops that successfully deal directly with consumers are food outlets, although many also handle hardware and drugs. Sales in this category were $1.3 billion in 1984 with only $19.1 million of that total generated in Ontario.[6]

Co-operatives and Wholesale

Retail co-ops can be served by either wholesale co-operatives or suppliers from the private sector. Similarly, co-op wholesalers provide private stores as well as co-op retailers with such products as fertilizer, building products, and gasoline. The four most prominent wholesalers are Federated Co-operatives Limited, United Co-operatives of Ontario, Co-op Atlantic, and Co-opérative Fédérée de Québec. These co-operatives are integrated backwards into manufacturing, running a number of lumber mills, plywood plants, and feed plants. The wholesale co-operatives are regionally based. For example, Federated Co-operatives is the creation of approximately 350 consumer and supply co-operatives situated in the West and serves as their central supplier. The sales of the wholesaler co-ops in 1984 varied from $1.3 billion for the western-based Federated Co-operatives to $269 million for the Atlantic group.[7]

GOVERNMENT OWNERSHIP: THE CASE OF LIQUOR DISTRIBUTION

Liquor Sales in Canada

After Prohibition, the provinces in Canada adopted liquor control policies which included government distribution systems.[8] The government liquor retailing complexes account for a substantial volume of sales. Representative sales for provinces from the different regions of Canada in the 1985–86 fiscal year were $1.65 billion for Ontario,[9] $936 million for Quebec,[10] $147 million for Newfoundland,[11] and $298 million for Saskatchewan.[12] Figures for the fiscal year ended in March 1985 by type of alcohol (spirits, wine, and beer) and for each province are presented in table 20. The composition of sales has been changing markedly. Typically, in the eighties, the volume of domestic and foreign spirits sold has fallen, and the sales volume of foreign wines has risen rapidly, while the volume of domestic wines has remained relatively constant and that of beer has grown at a modest rate.[13]

Table 20
Value of Liquor Sales by Province by Type for 1985
(in millions of dollars)

Province	Spirits	Wines	Beer	Total
Newfoundland	65	11	136	212
Prince Edward Island	18	3	19	40
Nova Scotia	116	29	130	274
New Brunswick	64	18	110	192
Quebec	446	434	806	1,687
Ontario	1,099	445	1,218	2,762
Manitoba	150	38	138	327
Saskatchewan	142	25	123	290
Alberta	394	120	343	857
British Columbia	425	214	404	1,044
Yukon	6	2	7	16
Northwest Territories	11	2	10	24
Total	2,936	1,343	3,445	7,724

Source: Statistics Canada, *The Control and Sale of Alcoholic Beverages in Canada, Fiscal Year ended March 31, 1985*, Ottawa, 1986, p. 24. Figures have been rounded.

The Network of Stores and Agents

All the government agencies operate chains of stores in their province. In Ontario there were 610 stores and in Newfoundland there were 37 stores directly under the control of their respective liquor boards in 1986. Within a chain, the sales of individual stores vary considerably. For instance, in Saskatchewan the store in the Broadway Shopping Centre in Regina sold $6,448,202 last year; in comparison, the store on Broadway Street in Saskatoon had sales of only $240,959.[14]

Many provinces designate agents to act on their behalf. In Ontario, the Brewers Warehousing Company, an industry-owned co-operative, has been granted the right to establish stores for the distribution of beer produced within the province. Membership in the co-operative consists of the larger breweries with Ontario production; they pay a fixed fee plus a share of current expenses. Smaller Ontario breweries who are not members can make arrangements to distribute their products through the 450 Brewers Retail stores.[15] Canadian breweries with production in other parts of the country must sell in Ontario through the regular outlets of the Liquor Control Board of Ontario (LCBO). Many provinces permit breweries to sell directly to taverns and other licensed on-premise retailers.

Although distribution practices are similar in each province, there is regional variation in the structure. Newfoundland permits its breweries to operate a retail outlet to service telephone orders. Manitoba licenses over 300 hotels to aid in the distribution of beer. The hotels can cheaply distribute the products largely through using existing personnel. They are required to take empties and are restricted to retailing domestic beer.[16] In Quebec, grocery stores with the required permits can sell beer that is made in the province, ciders, and wines that are bottled locally and approved by the Société des alcools du Québec (SAQ). In 1985–86 there were 11,356 *épiceries* licensed, in comparison to 9,018 in 1977–78. The SAQ also licenses certain wholesalers to sell the approved wines and ciders to the groceries.[17]

It is also common for the liquor commissions to serve small communities through agents. For instance, the Saskatchewan Liquor Board has 86 stores selling to the larger communities in the province and 159 special liquor vending outlets servicing such delightfully named spots as Cut Knife, Tramping Lake, and Porcupine Plain.[18] The LCBO services remote communities in Northern Ontario through agency arrangements with local concerns, such as tourist outfitters or food retailers. To be approved an outlet must have been in business for at least three years. The operators are required to charge LCBO prices but are allowed a 5 to 10 percent commission.[19]

Protecting Local Production from Foreigners and Other Canadians through the Distribution System

The protection of domestic production by the provinces through discriminatory retailing practices results in exports to foreign countries being more important than sales to other provinces. Moosehead beer, for example, is more readily available to its devotees in Los Angeles than it is in Ontario. The probability that beer would flow across provincial borders if the provincial selling agencies were not protectionist is revealed by examining the sales in Ontario or Quebec when there is a strike in the other province. In its 1969 annual report the LCBO attributed one-half of the increase in sales to the "unfortunate labour problems experienced by the Quebec Liquor Board during 1968." Under similar circumstances, the LCBO finds its imported beer sales also rise. For example, the sales volume of imported beer more than doubled between 1983/84 and 1984/85; the Board attributed this change to "the labour dispute which closed the major breweries in Ontario for most of March 1985."[20]

The two provinces with a significant capacity to grow grapes, Ontario and British Columbia, protect their wineries through special features of the distribution system.[21] Ontario, for example, permits provincial wineries to operate retail outlets. Historically, this practice began with the right of the winery to sell at its plant; the right was then made transferable to other sites. Rights could be accumulated through merger. In recent years there has been a dramatic increase in the number of winery-owned outlets. Although there were only 17 wineries in Ontario in 1986, there were 197 winery stores, 64 of which were self-contained areas in food or department stores.[22]

"Sin" Taxes

Liquor sales are a major source of revenue to the Canadian provinces and to the federal Treasury. In Ontario, for each bottle of imported table wine that sells for $5.90, the province receives $0.63 in sales tax and $2.97 in markup, for a total of $3.60. The federal government receives $0.25 in sales tax and $0.43 in excise duty. The producer of the product is paid $1.56 by the LCBO.[23] The proportional take of the government varies across products but is substantial for them all. For 1985/86, in Newfoundland over $75 million was paid to the provincial treasury and $25 million to the federal;[24] in Saskatchewan, the figures were $84 million and $44 million.[25] The two treasuries benefited by $802 million[26] and $339 million[27] respectively from operations by the Liquor Control Board of Ontario in 1985/86.[28] In addition, substantial provincial sales taxes are generated on alcohol sales. Some provinces levy a higher tax on alcohol sales than the standard sales tax. For example, Manitoba, which has a 6 percent sales tax, imposes a 12 percent levy on spirits, wine, and imported beer.[29] In addition, the issuing of licences and permits generates considerable revenue to the provincial governments.

Liquor Board Trade-Offs

The liquor boards face difficult trade-offs. They have a mandate to control the amount of liquor sold but also to market a product that many enjoy consuming and do so responsibly. They are also important generators of revenue for the government and are a potential source of protection for domestic producers. The marginal value of each of these objectives to the liquor board varies with the changing tastes of the public, the degree to which the public is informed, the capacity of private arrangements to deal with the externalities of the liquor trade[30] (e.g., the designated driver system), unemployment, and the deficit position of governments. With rising unemployment, changing social attitudes, and record deficits, it is predictable that the boards would increase their marketing efforts. By raising the effective demand the board can protect a little more, or raise a little more revenue, or relax controls, or some mix of the three.[31]

Government and Marketing

The marketing efforts have included the transition to self-serve outlets, albeit decades after the switch occurred in other areas of retail. In Ontario, 87 percent of the stores have been converted, and all will be by 1990.[32] In Saskatchewan, 78 of the 86 stores run by the liquor board are now self-serve.[33] The boards in many provinces are experimenting with restricted in-store promotions. For example, Manitoba in its 16 class "A" stores is permitting 21 displays for spirits and wines, 14 of which will be domestic and 7 foreign.[34] In 1985, the LCBO opened two boutique-style stores designed to create "an attractive and comfortable shopping environment." These "Vintages" stores provide a broad array of wines. The distance travelled since the fifties when customers slunk out of the grey-walled anti-boutiques with their brown bags is considerable. In the 1985/86 annual report, the LCBO enthusiastically discusses its new merchandising initiatives, referring to "industry end-aisle display programs, re-organized store layouts and generic product displays designed by store staff."

Despite these marketing efforts there is a uniformity to government retailing that is absent in private. In states like California that "contract out" liquor retailing to privately licensed outlets, the range of different styles of merchandising is of a different order of magnitude than that shown even in the more merchandising-aware liquor boards of the eighties. This tendency to uniformity in political distribution systems extends to pricing. Despite differences in costs, product is usually priced uniformly throughout the province. This apparent political imperative is revealed in the British Columbia experiment initiated on March 4, 1981, to allow more competition in the pricing of beer. Before that date, prices were set by the Minister of Consumer and Corporate Affairs for the province; after it, brewers could initiate price changes. However, a number of constraints on this price competition were imposed, including a requirement that the prices cannot vary geographically.[35]

A Schizophrenic Attitude to Advertising and Promotion

The conflict between control and marketing is also evident in the policies towards advertising by the liquor producers. All provinces have detailed provisions for regulating liquor advertising. Guidelines are published and prior notification of and approval by the board are necessary for running ads. In the case of broadcasting, the CRTCs regulations are adopted by many agencies. Some of the boards' guidelines are ambiguous and require subjective interpretation for their enforcement. For example, the Newfoundland code is typical in admonishing that:

> Advertising of alcoholic beverages will not make any claim that consumption of such beverages is beneficial to the user in any way nor shall it attempt to establish a certain product as a status symbol, a necessity for the enjoyment of life, nor an escape from life's problems nor shall it imply that consumption of such beverages is necessary for social prestige, business success, popularity with the opposite sex, or escape from personal problems.[36]

Presumably, the agencies try to reflect what they consider to be community tastes in exercising discretion on these matters. Another common clause that is impossible to enforce concerns the impact of advertising on total demand:

> Advertising may be used to instill brand preference, but must in no way be specifically designed to encourage the general consumption of alcoholic beverages or attempt to influence non-drinkers to drink.[37]

Are the beautiful people floating away from the beach in the colourful balloon promoting market share or increased consumption? A prohibition that any industry aspiring to form a cartel would love to have enforced by the government is the explicit or implicit prohibition of price advertising present in the regulatory codes. A licensing and taxing system, in contrast, could be made compatible with competition in pricing.

Licensing of On-Premise Outlets

The boards can influence alcohol demand by their marketing, by relaxing or tightening advertising regulations, and by influencing the cost of providing a complementary good. The complementary good that is under the control of the government is the right to serve liquor in taverns and at sports arenas, restaurants, bingos, et cetera. There are a number of categories of liquor licences issued for on-premise consumption. The categories in Saskatchewan (with the number in effect at March 31, 1985) for example, are restaurants (7), hotel beverage rooms (496), restaurant beverage rooms (6), dining rooms (559), cocktail rooms (309), clubs (108), and canteens (75).[38] In most jurisdictions, the licensee buys the product from the boards at list price. The licences are themselves a source of funds to the government. In 1985/86, $267,202,779 was collected for the Ontario treasury on account of licence fees and permits.[39]

Vertical Integration

Just as is the case in private retailing, vertical integration into manufacturing occurs in the liquor trade. The liquor boards bottle a number of products and retail them under their labels. Ontario produces a popular set of Spanish sherries and selected liquors, but perhaps the most ambitious in this regard is the SAQ. By percentage of volume, the wines bottled by the SAQ have represented about 30 percent of its sales of wines in the past five years.[40]

The Labour Force and Sharing Monopoly Rents

The government liquor stores hire a large proportion of part-time help, as do many operations in the private retail trade. The Saskatchewan board reports that it has 300 full-time employees and 293 part-time.[41] The Manitoba board has a similar profile, with 115 full-time store clerks, 61 full-time assistant managers, 49 liquor store managers, and 233 part-time employees. The labour force is highly unionized in comparison to private retailing. The average weekly earnings for all employees in liquor, wine, and beer stores was $383, for all salaried employees $560, and for employees paid by the hour $343 in August of 1987. These were substantially higher than the earnings for the same groups working in other retail outlets. The equivalent averages for retail as a whole in the same month were $273, $406 and $218.[42] It is difficult to believe that the premiums of 29 percent, 38 percent, and 57 percent result from additional skills, training, or education required in this line of sales as compared to others. A far more plausible explanation is that some of the monopoly rents are shared with liquor, wine, and beer store employees at the expense of the general tax-payer.

As far as gender employment is concerned, the government liquor boards have been traditionally male preserves. With recent concerns about gender discrimination, the boards have been striving to alter the mix of employees. In Manitoba, for example, 77 percent of the full-time store clerks are men, while 55 percent of the part-time help are men.[43] Charges of discrimination under the Human Rights Code have also been made against the boards. For example, in 1985, three employees of the LCBOs quality-control laboratory filed charges that they had been discriminated against on racial grounds.[44]

Licensing Retail Outlets

In a world of costless transactions, the revenue generating capacity of a taxation and licensing scheme should be equivalent to that of a government monopoly. Because of the different motivations of a private versus a government run system, the outcome would be expected to differ in a world where monitoring and enforcement are costly.[45] In addition, large government monopolies can exert monopsonistic power in buying. Private buyers can also do this if they act in concert, but concerted action can also be used to raise prices and impose damages on consumers.

A provincial government also has an incentive to adopt a government monopoly because it can capture revenue which would have to be shared with the federal government under a system of licensing and taxing private firms. This diversion occurs because the federal corporate income tax doesn't apply to the control board's "profits." More subtly, the political equilibrium tends to differ between licensing jurisdictions and monopoly ones, because of a private ownership interest in those with licensing and a bureaucratic one in monopoly jurisdictions. In a jurisdiction that opts for licensing, some of the potential "tax" may be levied in terms of "donations" to the competing parties. In our opinion, the decision about which regime to adopt depends on how Canadians assess the enterprise and innovation inspired by the profit system net of the "costs" of channelling the initiatives in benign directions.

Although some states in the United States have fully privatized liquor distribution, no province in Canada has taken this route. The agency arrangements represent a partial privatization, and adjustment is constantly occurring in terms of the amount of trade that is being "contracted out" through the agents. Groups like small groceries will continue to lobby for the right to be designated agents for some products.[46] There would appear to be every reason to consider the licensing-out option; there would appear to be no reason to limit eligibility for the right to one group of merchants.

In examining the licensing-out option, special attention will have to be paid to the problem of crafting enforceable terms which are consistent with the control mandate of the government. Can we constrain the negative externalities from drinking[47] while providing incentives for people to develop more imaginative retailing of the products?

Alternatively, can government agencies become better retailers? We think that the potential in this direction is limited. The problem is not one of management but of constraints. A government retail agency is under political pressure to provide the same service to all communities that have similar broad statistical profiles.[48] The focus of a private system of retail is to discover and serve the differences that lie within even apparently homogeneous communities. The weakness of the private system in this context is that the profit incentive encourages licensees to obey the letter of control constraints but seek ways around them. Loophole mining for putting up larger signs, staying open longer, expanding floor space, and using more questionable merchandising practices becomes an important preoccupation of management. The challenge for the politicians is to find a "governance structure,"[49] a mix of constraints, enforcement mechanisms, and private arrangements, within which these two objectives can be reconciled. Conceptually, the problem is similar to that addressed by shopping centres and franchise arrangements, which are discussed in the next chapter.

NOTES

1. The authors are unaware of any empirical studies comparing performance for co-ops and commercial firms in the Canadian trade sector.

2. The stipulations in the Acts are quite detailed. For example, the Saskatchewan Act Respecting Co-operatives is 142 pages long.

3. Co-operative Union of Canada, *Co-operatives Canada '86*, p. 21.

4. Ibid., p. 21.

5. R.J. McSween, *A History of Nova Scotia Co-operatives* (Nova Scotia Department of Agriculture and Marketing 1985) pp. 3-4.

6. *Co-operation in Canada 1984*, July 1986, p. 34. For Prairie shares of co-operatives in food see table 17.

7. Co-operative Union of Canada, *Co-operatives Canada '86*, p. 23.

8. In Canada, Prohibition was enacted in 1917 on a national level. Prior to that date, municipalities could prohibit the retailing of liquor under the Temperance Act, first enacted in 1884. British Columbia and Quebec went "wet" in 1921, but Prince Edward Island did not do so until after the Second World War. In the United States a similar evolution occurred, although the dates do not overlap exactly. One difference that is important for retailing is that after Prohibition a number of American states opted to control liquor sales through taxing and licensing of private wholesalers and retailers rather than through government monopolies.

9. Liquor Control Board of Ontario, *60th Report*, April 1st to March 31st 1986, p. 4.

10. La société des Alcoöls du Québec, *Rapport Annuel 1985-86*, p. 9.

11. Newfoundland Liquor Corporation, *1986 Annual Report*, p. 6.

12. Saskatchewan Liquor Board, *Annual Report 1985-86*, p. 31.

13. To illustrate with the Ontario experience between 1981-82 and 1985-86: the volume of Canadian and foreign spirit sales fell from 40 percent of the total to 33.3 percent; Canadian wines fell from 17.4 percent of total volume to 16.7 percent, while foreign wine sales grew from 20 percent to 24.2 percent of total volume. Over the same period, beer sales rose from 22.6 percent to 25.3 percent of total volume. During the five-year period, the total volume increased at a modest rate of less than 0.5 percent per year, from a level of over 180 million litres to

close to 186 million litres. See Liquor Control Board of Ontario, *60th Report*, April 1st to March 31st 1986.

14. Data are from the annual reports of the liquor boards cited.

15. The information was provided in a letter from the Ontario Minister of Consumer and Commercial Relations, Monte Kwinter, dated June 12, 1987.

16. This information was provided to us by the Manitoba Liquor Commission.

17. Information provided by the Régie des permis d'alcool of the province of Quebec.

18. Saskatchewan Liquor Board, *Annual Report 1985-86*, p. 6 and p. 10.

19. The information was provided in a letter from the Ontario Minister of Consumer and Commercial Relations, Monte Kwinter, dated June 12, 1987, p. 4.

20. Liquor Control Board of Ontario, *60th Report*, April 1st to March 31st 1986.

21. British Columbia recently permitted a drugstore, London Drugs, in North Vancouver, to sell wine, wine-based coolers, and cider supplied by Andres Wines of Port Moody. The British Columbia government is committed to relaxing its sales policies for these products.

22. Liquor Control Board of Ontario, *60th Report*, April 1st to March 31st 1986, p. 17.

23. Liquor Control Board of Ontario, *60th Report*, April 1st to March 31st 1986, p. 9.

24. Newfoundland Liquor Corporation, *1986 Annual Report*, p. 7 for provincial figure. Federal figure is derived by applying the percentage given on p. 3 to the revenue obtained from p. 7.

25. Saskatchewan Liquor Board, *Annual Report 1985-86*, p. 34 and p. 38 respectively.

26. This figure does not include the over $117 million collected in retail sales tax on sales through Brewers Retail stores and through winery stores. It is the sum of provincial sales tax collected through LCBO stores, $164 million, and the profits remitted by the LCBO, $638 million. See Liquor Control Board of Ontario, *60th Report*, April 1st to March 31st 1986, p. 8.

27. This figure is composed of $258 million in customs and excise duty and $80 million in federal sales tax. It excludes over $252 million paid in malt duties and taxes on domestic beers and wines. See Liquor Control Board of Ontario, *60th Report,* April 1st to March 31st 1986, p. 8.

28. Figures are for 1986 and are derived from the annual reports of the liquor agencies in those provinces.

29. Statistics Canada, *The Control and Sale of Alcoholic Beverages in Canada, Fiscal Year ended March 31, 1985* (Ottawa, 1986) p. 6.

30. The negative effects that are most frequently mentioned in the literature are fatalities from accidents involving alcohol, decreased productivity, absenteeism, illness (the connection between cirrhosis and alcohol appears to be well-founded, although cirrhosis can occur in non-drinkers), and strife or violence in the home and public places. Some of the direct effects are borne primarily by the individual, and society is affected through the fiscal externalities caused by the strain on the medical insurance schemes, the legal system, welfare programmes, and the like. Inference of cause to alcohol for many of these effects can be disputed. A good discussion of the problems appears in D. Gerstein, "Programmes, Interests and Alcohol," ch. 3 in Marcus Grant, Martin Plant and Alan Williams (eds.), *Economics and Alcohol* (Gardiner Press Inc. 1983). Gerstein still concludes that "the evidence is persuasive that alcohol misuse generates a remarkable amount of trouble in the United States, and that the overall social interest in maintaining and improving measures to reduce this amount is substantial" (p. 61). There are also many positive socializing effects of the use of alcohol. We suspect that in Canada its use creates a lot of pleasure and a lot of trouble and that we will continue to grope for better governance structures for its distribution and use.

31. That government revenue rises when the tax rate increases requires the revenue curve to be inelastic at the equilibrium. The government may perceive the spillover effects to be sufficiently severe to warrant prohibition, in which case legal production and tax revenue are zero, and presumably no promotion takes place.

32. Liquor Control Board of Ontario, *60th Report,* April 1st to March 31st 1986, p. 16.

33. Saskatchewan Liquor Board, *Annual Report 1985-86,* p. 7.

34. Manitoba Liquor Commission, Brand Display Programme.

35. For an account of the changes and their effects see C. Eckel and M. Goldberg, "Regulation and Deregulation of the Brewing Industry: the British Columbia Example," *Canadian Public Policy*, X (1984). They also point out that the restriction puts regional breweries at a competitive disadvantage, (see p. 323).

36. Newfoundland Liquor Corporation, Newfoundland Advertising Code.

37. Ibid.

38. Saskatchewan Liquor Licensing Commission, *Annual Report 1984-1985*, p. 6.

39. Liquor Control Board of Ontario, *60th Report*, April 1st to March 31st 1986, p. 8.

40. For statistics from 1978/79 to 1982/83 see Gouvernement du Québec, Ministère de l'Industrie et du Commerce, *Profil de l'Industrie et du Commerce des Boissons Alcoöliques au Québec* (1985) tableau 5, p. 23.

41. Saskatchewan Liquor Board, *Annual Report 1985-86*, p. 5.

42. Figures are from Statistics Canada, *Employment, Earnings and Hours*, September 1987 preliminary data (December 1987) p. 46.

43. Manitoba data are from correspondence with the Liquor Commission of that province.

44. See *Globe and Mail*, Sept. 28, 1985, article with headline "LCBO Accused of Racist Promotion Practices."

45. A private system may show more initiative in increasing sales and thereby the base for taxes. It will also show more initiative in reducing the effective tax rate to divert income from public coffers to the enterprise. An early article by Julian Simon concluded that monopoly states raise more revenue and have lower prices than their licensing counterparts ("The Economics Effects of State Monopoly of Package-Liquor Retailing," *Journal of Political Economy*, 74 (1966)). The differences in political equilibria have been addressed in some recent work, such as Eugenia Toma, "State Liquor Licensing and Dry/Wet Counties," (mimeo 1987) and Carlos Seiglie, "A Theory of the Politically Optimal Commodity Tax" (mimeo 1987).

46. They have obtained this right in Quebec.

47. The negative externalities, such as drunk driving, can be attacked through changes in age restrictions and in criminal and tort law, but there are limits to the efficacy of this approach as well. (Cf. H. Ross, "Deterrence of the Drinking Driver: An International Survey," Law and Economics Workshop series, University of Toronto, wsIII-5 undated). The fiscal externalities on the medical insurance system could be reduced by altering the affected scheme. The authors have not analysed the effect of such changes but note that a dramatic change in regime would probably require alterations in these interrelated areas of policy.

48. One example is noted by Catherine C. Eckel and M.A. Goldberg, "Regulation and Deregulation of the Brewing Industry: The British Columbia Example," *Canadian Public Policy*, X:3, with respect to the marketing of beer in British Columbia. "In B.C., a further regulation requires that every product be available for sale province-wide, with resulting high distribution costs for low-volume products" (p. 317).

49. A felicitous expression coined by O.E. Williamson, "Transaction Cost Economics: The Governance of Contractual Relations," *Journal of Law and Economics*, 22 (Oct. 1979).

Chapter 7

ORGANIZATIONAL UMBRELLAS: FRANCHISES AND SHOPPING CENTRES

INTRODUCTION

The focus of this chapter is the private governance structures under which the activities of different organizations within the trade sector are co-ordinated. In particular, the arrangements between a franchisor and franchisee and the co-ordinating role of the shopping centre are analysed.

Franchising

Franchising has been a rapidly growing means of retailing. The *Financial Post*[1] estimates that by 1990 over 50 percent of the retail market will be franchised. Between 1981 and 1984, the growth rate in franchises exceeded 15 percent.

Franchising Agreements

Franchising embraces a reasonably wide range of relationships between a franchisor and franchisee. The distinctive features of the arrangements are: (a) the franchisor has brand name capital in a product line or in a product line plus the ancillary retailing techniques; (b) inputs are required by the franchisee and franchisor which are difficult for the other party to monitor; and (c) the payments structure, which typically involves an up-front payment by the franchisee and royalty fees calculated as a percentage of sales, is designed to reward the franchisor for the brand capital and reduce the costs imposed by the monitoring problem.

Although there are many variants, franchise contracts cluster around two types, traditional and business franchises. Traditional franchises are less restrictive and give more managerial freedom to the franchisee. Automobile dealers and service station operators are representative of this type of franchise. In contrast, in business franchises much greater control is exerted over the franchisee's method of operation, over logo display and, particularly for retail, over the presentation of merchandise. The statistics on franchising are fragmentary. In the data for the period 1976 to 1981, presented in table 21, it is apparent that traditional franchises are growing less rapidly than business franchises.

Table 21

Franchising in the Canadian Economy

(billions of dollars in sales)

	1976	1977	1978	1979	1980	1981
Aggregate	20.1	22.1	25.9	31.8	38.9	46.8
Retail	1.2	1.4	1.6	2.0	2.6	3.2
Traditional Franchises*	15.2	16.3	18.4	21.0	22.1	24.7

Source: From Statistics Canada, *Market Research Handbook 1985-86*, 63-224, table 2-16, p. 129, February 1986. (There are no notes to this table in the handbook, but the reader is notified to contact the statistical agency. Contact with the agency as suggested revealed that the figures in the handbook which were reported as millions of dollars were sales figures and should have been in billions. We were also told that these figures were generated by a unique survey and that more current data on this topic are not available.)

Note: * Motor vehicle dealers, service stations and soft drink bottlers.

A Hierarchy of Arrangements

There are different tiers at which franchise arrangements can be made. A franchisor may deal directly with franchisees who operate individual outlets. Alternatively, the franchisor can grant a multiple-unit franchise contract[2] that gives the holder the right to make arrangements with a number of sub-franchises. These tiered contracts are particularly attractive when the franchisor is trying to tap a new market which is culturally, legally, or linguistically different from the home market. This arrangement permits the holder some degree of freedom to adapt the concept to the local market.

Under a master franchising contract the

"franchisor receives initial franchise fees from the master franchisee, as well as a portion of the initial franchise fees paid by the sub-franchisees to the master franchisee. In addition, the franchisor receives a portion of the continuing royalty fees paid by each sub-franchisee to the master franchisee."[3]

Obligations and Rights

A typical franchise contract contains a number of stipulations. In almost all cases, the franchisor is required to give managerial assistance. This assistance encompasses aid in selecting a site, advice in running training programmes for employees, the provision of standard operating manuals, design of the physical layout of the retail establishment, advertising layout advice, and general operating information. The franchisee in turn agrees to controls over the products sold, price, hours of operation, conditions of the store, inventory levels, details of its maintenance, insurance, personnel, and accounting and auditing systems.

The franchisee also agrees to pay royalties, usually based on sales. In Canada the average is 5 percent across franchises of all types, but it varies with the type of business and from franchisor to franchisor. The franchisee may also be required to buy inputs from the franchisor or from a supplier chosen from a specified list. A franchise contract usually has a termination clause which permits the franchisor to terminate the contract at will. On the other hand, the franchisee is bound for a longer period of time, typically 10 to 20 years. In the interim, the right of the franchisee to transfer the franchise to another party is usually circumscribed. Some arrangements permit heirs to inherit the business but generally the right can only be transferred with approval of the franchisor. The contract will often restrict the right of the franchisee to establish a similar business in the area after ceasing to be a franchisee. In some contracts, the franchisee will receive rights to an exclusive area. Often the franchisee is required to pay a percentage of sales to support advertising by the franchisor.[4] These fees average 2 percent of sales in Canada. In addition, a business franchisee is required to pay an up-front fee. In the traditional franchise arrangements, an up-front fee may not be required.[5] Under both franchise arrangements, the franchisee will make investments in local facilities.

Matching Franchisor and Franchisees

The franchisor reinforces the incentive effects of the contract by screening potential franchisees, in order to identify those who are least likely to be opportunistic. The length of the queue of aspiring franchisees will be influenced by the generosity of the sharing terms within the contract. Consultants have sprung up to help the franchisor in the task of choosing among the applicants. Franchise Services Inc. is one group specializing in matching franchisees and franchisors. Potential franchisees pay $15 to be registered with the firm, and the list of potential franchisees is made available to franchisors. If a match is made the chain is charged $250. They also have developed and administer the Zee Evaluation, which assesses potential franchisees. According to the firm the "ideal franchisee blends the ebullience of a salesman with the willingness of a soldier to take orders."6 One of its franchisor clients stated that they also consider financing and experience and place a weight on the test results of between 15 and 20 percent.

Internal Mechanisms to Resolve Conflicts

Settling contract disputes through legal action is costly, and many franchisors encourage the creation of councils of franchisees to provide a forum for settling disputes, for modifying arrangements where it is mutually advantageous, and for exchanging information. Canadian Tire, for example, has a Dealers' Association that has the formal objective "to help the combined Dealer/Home Office organization prosper." An enlightening example of the value of a council is provided by Kettle Creek Canvas Co., a Port Stanley, Ontario, franchisor of heavy duty sportswear outlets with 30 franchisees. A five-member committee acts as franchise council for the chain. Kettle Creek did not have a clause in its franchise contract providing for dunning franchisees to pay for national advertising. It became evident to the franchisees that having a joint advertising campaign would raise their profits. The Kettle Creek group representing the *franchisees* organized a national programme paid for by a voluntary 4 percent levy. The campaign was successful, but it did not have 100 percent participation in 1986; the second campaign, however, has received 100 percent support.[7]

Economic Explanation of Contract Structure

Economists have been interested in the reasons why the franchise contract has some of its features.[8] Why is an up-front franchise fee levied and why does the franchisor share in the profits of the franchisee through royalty fees? In his study, Frank Mathewson emphasizes that innovations in media, particularly the advent of television, made brand names cheaper to develop and encouraged the growth of franchised chains, as well as chains of corporately owned stores. His empirical work shows that franchising and television advertising are correlated. The organizational problem is to fashion a franchise contract that creates incentives for the franchisee to provide the inputs that complement the brand name capital developed by the franchisor.

The up-front fee, the sharing attributes, and the right to terminate by the franchisor provide incentives that reduce the amount of free-riding by both the franchisee and the franchisor. The hazard faced by the franchisee is well illustrated by the comments of Ned Levitt, a lawyer, reported in a recent *Financial Post* that dedicated a section to the franchising phenomenon:

> The franchisee puts up the front money, thinking it will buy good training, help with selecting a location [and other special skills needed to get going]. But what's really being financed is the franchisor's lifestyle. He simply isn't putting enough of the front load back into the system to make the system grow and work.[9]

The hazard faced by the franchisor is revealed by the experiences of the Singer Sewing Machine Co., which was the first to develop franchise arrangements in the United States during the nineteenth century but used an incomplete contract by modern standards. According to one account, the Singer initiative failed because the company granted an overly generous share to the franchisees along with exclusive territorial rights and did not include a termination clause:

> In some territories dealers proved lazy or inefficient, allowing rival companies to steal sales. Singer could do nothing to prevent this. Under their contract, dealers had exclusive rights to their territories. The company could not withdraw these rights or send in salaried representatives.[10]

Over time, a franchise contract has evolved which is better structured to create and maintain the wealth that can be generated by the joint efforts of the franchisee and the franchisor. It does so by including provisions which ensure a reduction in profit that would be greater than the money value of shirking on assumed responsibilities.

Franchises Versus Company-Owned Outlets

A retail chain faces a similar problem in co-ordinating its activities and those of its store manager to that faced by a franchisor with an "independent" franchisee. Accordingly, we should expect that the employee contract has many of the same features as the franchise contract. The principal difference between a company-owned store and a franchise arrangement is the up-front fee received from a franchisee. The company employee in charge of a company-owned store can be and usually is rewarded on a basis contingent on performance. For example, the managerial contract in company-owned stores at Radio Shack has a low base pay and substantial bonuses based on store profits. Similarly, a franchisee can be restrained to behave like a company employee in his or her operations by the details of the franchise contract. Another difference, in addition to the absence of an up-front payment, is the ability within an integrated company to issue new instructions to a manager in a situation which is not covered by the present instructions; under franchising the new specifications must be negotiated. Alternatively, if some action by the franchisee is not explicitly forbidden, the franchisor must persuade (reward) the franchisee to alter his or her behaviour.[11]

The margin at which the profit potential of two organizational forms is the same is revealing. Most franchisors have both company-owned stores and franchised outlets. One would expect that the less important and the more routine the input of the local store operator, the closer the outlets to the head office of the chain, and the more densely located the outlets, the more likely is company ownership. For the two retail chains covered by a Laventhol & Horwath survey, St. Clair Paint & Wallpaper and The Kiddie Kobbler, the company-owned versus franchised outlets were 48/124 and 3/60 respectively. For the Radio Shack chain on a world-wide level the recent count was 5,700 corporate stores and 3,000 franchised.[12] The shift in this margin in gasoline marketing was previously discussed.

Many large chains are constantly adjusting the margin by buying franchises back or selling corporate stores to franchisees. For example, Kelley Douglas, the western food distributor that is 67 percent owned by Weston, sold its corporate stores to franchisees in British Columbia in 1979. On many occasions, such shifts reflect the changing efficiency of the different modes of contracting. In other cases, the change may be dictated by a pecuniary saving which is not necessarily reflecting a resource saving. In the food industry, Don Collins, of the Retail, Wholesale and Department Stores Union, expressed a concern that, at least in some instances, franchising was a way of breaking union contracts that had been negotiated with corporate stores.

Government Policy and Franchises

Most of the Canadian provinces have not passed special legislation to cover franchising; they rely on contract law as a regulator of the activity. The exception is Alberta which, under the Franchises Act, requires a franchisor to register and file a prospectus which includes a brief history of the operation and its personnel and summaries of obligations and rights in the contract, including the help that the franchisee can expect to receive from the franchisor. A financial statement of the franchisor and a copy of the franchise agreement must also be submitted. The Alberta Securities Commission states that it will review applications and comment on them within ten days of receipt. There is a filing fee of $250, and a surety bond will be required if the franchisor has no assets in the province of Alberta. The amount of the surety bond is determined by the Securities Commission.

Since the legislation is recent, it is difficult to determine the extent to which the Alberta Franchise Act has either prevented abuses that retard the expansion of beneficial franchise arrangements or acted as an impediment to achieving that purpose. Its disclosure and bonding requirements could help redress the informational disadvantage of the franchisee, but the detailed disclosure requirements may also pose threats to the intellectual property capital of the franchisor and thereby deter franchisors from entering the provincial market.

The new federal Competition Act may also have an impact on franchising. Kenneth Fong of McDonald's Restaurants of Canada Limited has noted the ambiguity of whether the granting of a franchise is covered by the new merger provisions of the act. He is concerned with the impact of the law in the following situation:

> A franchisor determines that a given market area will support an additional franchised outlet. The existing franchisee in that market area wishes to obtain those franchise rights and, in the opinion of the franchisor, is "expandable." However, a "qualified" third party applies for the franchise rights for that location. Can the franchisor proceed with confidence and grant the franchise in the face of the real possibility that the rejected third party may complain that a grant of franchise "is likely to lessen competition substantially"?[13]

Mr. Fong is also concerned that the prenotification requirement for substantive mergers in the new Act will apply in the case of a large franchisor buying back a substantial sub-franchisor under a master franchise agreement plan. The ambiguity of the connection between franchise contracts and the Competition Act will not be resolved until test cases have been tried.

The Incidence of Franchising in Retail

Franchises are ubiquitous in the food sector. The food distributors controlled by George Weston Ltd., for example, had 1,350 franchised stores in 1981. According to a survey taken by the Association of Canadian Franchisors,[14] average sales for a franchisor in the food sector ranged from a high of $2.5 billion to a low of $200,000 per annum. The average food franchisor had 24 outlets and sales averaged $175,000 at each. Initial franchise fees ranged from $20,000 to $29,000. Average total investment by a franchisee was $145,000, while royalty fees were higher than for franchises in other sectors and averaged $20,000 per year. The mean employment per franchisor was 189, greater than in any other area of franchising.

Franchises are also popular in the non-food retail sector, in particular for clothing, shoe, drug, paint and wallpaper, video rental, and computer stores. Average sales for a franchisor in this sector were $4.1 million. The average number of units in a chain was 27, and average sales per unit were $152,000. The mean initial franchise fee was $11,250, the lowest for any type of business franchise. Total investment averaged $105,000 per franchise.

For business franchises as a whole the survey showed that over 80 percent of all employees were working part-time. Another claim that is made for franchise arrangements is that the incidence of bankruptcy is much less than for independent entrants.[15]

One of the largest retail franchisors is Canadian Tire, which had 375 associated stores in 1983, an increase of 88 stores from the figure a decade earlier. These stores are spread across all ten Canadian provinces. As its advertisements claim, Canadian Tire stores sell much more than tires; its outlets carry a unique blend of automotive equipment, hardware, sporting goods, kitchen supplies, and small appliances. The sharing contracts typical of the relationship between a franchisor and franchisee have been extended in this organization to the employees; Canadian Tire has one of the most ambitious profit-sharing plans in Canada for its employees, paying $10.4 million to employees in profit-sharing awards in 1983.

Canadian Tire began franchising in the 1930s. An example of a more recent entrant into the field is the British Columbia franchisor Work World Enterprises, which specializes in work clothes. The founder, Bernie Bielby, was an employee of Sears for 18 years before embarking on this enterprise. The chain now has 58 stores. The up-front franchise fee is $25,000 and other initial costs are about $55,000. The royalty fee is 3.5 percent of sales. Some franchisees have reported earning as much as $100,000 a year.[16]

International Franchising and Canada

The Canadian market has been an important area of expansion for American franchisors. Recently, American franchising has grown even more rapidly in Europe and Asia. Canada's share of foreign franchises by American franchisors actually fell from 46 percent in 1971 to 31 percent in 1982.[17]

Similarly, the American market has been the first market considered when Canadian franchisors have been contemplating foreign expansion. However, this expansion has been relatively modest in the retail sector, particularly in comparison to the expansion abroad of Canadian retailing through the purchase of existing foreign chains. As examples, the St. Clair Paint & Wallpaper chain has 172 outlets in Canada and 4 in the United

States, while children's shoe retailer Kiddie Kobbler Ltd. has 63 Canadian stores and 3 abroad. According to a survey by Laventhol & Horwath commissioned by the Department of Regional Industrial Expansion (DRIE), the main impediments to foreign expansion by Canadian franchisors were: the difficulty of identifying suitable franchisees and of selling themselves where they don't have a track record; legal, regulatory, and financial complications; trademark licensing and copyright difficulties; foreign exchange conversion problems; taxation uncertainties; zoning restrictions; import controls, and customs entanglements experienced in sending furniture and fixtures to foreign markets.[18] Nevertheless, in the survey by the Association of Canadian Franchisors, 50 percent of the respondents indicated that they planned to expand abroad.

When Canadian franchisors expand abroad they often begin by establishing a company-owned store rather than a franchised outlet, in order to become informed about the business environment in the new setting. After becoming informed the franchisor is in a better position to advise any future franchisee and can also adapt the franchising contract to reflect the local conditions. A successful company-owned store also has a positive demonstration effect as far as potential franchisees are concerned.

The Lack of Incentives for Organizational Innovation

The evolution of the trade sector illustrates that organizational developments have been critical in developing better retailing and wholesaling. Unlike product innovation, organizational breakthroughs cannot be patented. The originators do not receive a temporary legal monopoly as inventors do. It is certainly arguable that the development of the modern decentralized corporation did as much for our wellbeing as the invention of the phonograph. An organizational innovator can reap economic rents from being first in the field, and perhaps this gives a sufficient incentive for innovation in this area, but if the rents are significant, imitators are attracted in a hurry. This is certainly the case with franchised clothing stores in North America. Consider San Francisco's Banana Republic, which developed a unique "urban safari" product line and a marketing style. Its immense success has attracted a number of imitators with nearly identical products, matching ambience, and similar names.[19]

Shopping Malls

In 1951 there were only four shopping centres in Canada; in 1987, a small town would have that many. In Ottawa alone, there are now 69 shopping centres, with 4.7 million square feet of shopping space, a quarter of which have been developed since 1980.[20]

The Shopping Centre Spectrum

Shopping centres are commonly classified by size into three categories: neighbourhood, community and regional. A typical neighbourhood shopping centre has 5 to 15 outlets and 50,000 square feet of floor space. Independent stores and local chains are disproportionately represented, as are beer and liquor outlets. Community shopping centres are about three times as large as the neighbourhood type. A large proportion of their sales is generated by supermarkets, convenience stores, and for the larger ones in this classification, a junior department store.

All shopping centres larger than 250,000 square feet are classified as regional shopping centres. They are often covered malls and are anchored by one or more senior or junior department stores. Grocery sales are a lower percentage of total sales in these complexes. A large proportion of their sales is generated by the department stores and by the national non-food chains. The reliance of chains on shopping centre outlets is high, ranging from a high of 55.7 percent for women's clothing to a low of 4.3 percent for general merchandising stores.[21] In 1956, there were only six regional shopping centres in Canada. By 1982 they were ubiquitous; in St. John's, Newfoundland, alone, there were two regional centres, each with a floor area of approximately 600,000 square feet.

To illustrate the range in number of stores, leasable space, annual volume, rent, and other charges, data from a sample of the 40 shopping centres in the Ottawa area are reproduced in table 22. Rents rise with the number of stores, the leasable area, and the location of the centre. The relative importance of rent, maintenance charges, and percentages of gross varies considerably from centre to centre.

Large real estate developers have been active in developing shopping centres, often in conjunction with housing and office space projects. In addition, many of the large department store chains have become involved in shopping centre development. The American parent of K mart, a prominent junior department chain with stores in each province of Canada, reported in its 1983 annual report:

> Today, K mart the retailer is frequently also K mart the developer. While most K mart properties were once built and managed by independent developers, K mart now often serves as landlords as well as tenant.

> Through the new K mart Development Division, real estate and construction associates follow selected K mart shopping centre projects from concept to opening day. K mart staff identifies sites; obtains proper zoning; civic approvals and financing; acquires property; selects contractors and oversees construction; funds other tenants and manages the properties after the centers open.[22]

Table 22
Rentals and Charges for Selected Ottawa Area Shopping Centres

	Number of Stores	Gross Leasable Area	Annual Volume (millions of $)	Average Rent / Foot ($)	Common Charge / Foot ($)	Average Percent of Gross
Barhaven Mall	29	45,000	10–15	12	2.5	6
Bayshore*	103	655,000	93	40–50	na	6–8
Beacon Hill	20	109,000	10–25	8	6	7
Bells Corners	3	120,000	10	6	na	5
Billings Bridge Plaza	120	460,000	70–75	25	3.75	7
Blackburn Shoppes	18	54,000	8	13	1.87	6
Blossum Park	7	125,000	10	10	na	5
Convent Glen	30	100,000	na	18	2	8
Hunt Club	10	70,000	na	10	1.8	8
Ikea	9	84,000	30–35	9	3.36	5
K Mart Plaza (Nepean)	8	117,000	10–15	10–15	na	6–8
K Mart Plaza (Ottawa)	6	120,000	30–35	6	2	na
Kanata Town	17	91,000	na	12	1.2	8
Lincoln Heights	50	296,000	50–75	18	4.5	6
McArthur Plaza	19	64,000	10–15	10	1	6
Merivale Shopping	18	72,000	1–5	12	6.81	5
Montreal Square	11	63,000	na	9	3.85	6–8
Shopper City East	24	171,000	31–36	7–20	na	1–7
Shopper City West	25	169,000	31–36	5–20	na	1–7
Westgate	30	142,000	25–27	25–27	na	6

Source: The data are from *Annual Inventory of Shopping Centres 1987*, Maclean Hunter (Toronto: 1987). Only those shopping centres which provided data for five out of the six categories are reproduced in table 18.

Note: * Excludes the Bay and Eaton's.

In Canada, a concern of the regions has been the flow of funds to real estate firms or developers located in central Canada. In response to this concern, Prince Edward Island became involved in ownership in one mall in Summerside and a department store in Charlottetown. The Prince Edward Island commission on shopping centres advised the province to abandon this more activist role in retailing.[23]

Canadian firms also own a considerable number of shopping centres in the United States. For example, in taking over Allied, Robert Campeau acquired a 50 percent interest in 5 million square feet of American shopping centre space.

Co-ordinating Activities within the Shopping Centre

A shopping centre is an interesting phenomenon. It is an umbrella organization under which the complementary offerings of competing stores, restaurants, leisure services, and parking are co-ordinated in order to provide an enhanced package to the shopper. A store manager allocates space among different product lines and places each line strategically in a store; similarly, the shopping centre co-ordinator allocates space and places different types of stores strategically within a centre.

The co-ordination involves choosing not only store types and appropriate rental charges, but also architectural aspects and operational ones such as the determination of hours of service. The shopping centre manager will be the spear carrier in lobbying for the interests of the group with respect to zoning, transportation, and security. He or she is a town planner on a small scale, studying traffic flows within the complex and judging the optimal amount of space that should be concourse (roads), how much should be reserved for rest areas (parks), and how much should be directly income-producing (commercially zoned). The motivation is to raise the profit being derived from the retailing complex.

Internalizing Externalities

In the jargon of economics, a shopping centre allows some externalities to be internalized. An economically relevant externality occurs if there is scope to alter an action so both the actor and others affected can benefit.[24] An externality reflects a forgone gain from better co-ordination. A shopping centre removes some externalities; it raises wealth by co-ordinating store offerings. It is in the interest of each store to accept the combination of rents and restrictions, if it makes more money than it could elsewhere. In this sense, a shopping centre arrangement is a complex contract, like a franchise arrangement, that enhances co-ordination.

Reducing Search Costs and Increasing Competition

A shopping centre also offers its clients a reduction in search costs and some assurance of competition within the complex. Except for the neighbourhood centres, shopping centres encourage multiple outlets for different types of merchandise. In Ottawa the downtown Rideau Centre has three department stores, Eaton's, the Bay, and Ogilvy's, and all the regional centres in the area have at least two. The Yorkdale complex which opened in Toronto in 1964 was the first in which Simpsons and Eaton's stores appeared in the same centre. Eaton's had owned the land on which the complex was built. Asked about the decision to include Simpsons in the project, Mr. Kinnear, the CEO of Eaton's at the time, noted, "It's an axiom of retailing that two big stores near each other attract more than twice as many customers as they would singly."[25] Internal competition may also make monitoring easier for the owner of the shopping centre. If one shoe store is not doing well, that fact will be evident if there are three others to compare it with.[26]

Differential Rents as an Instrument of Co-ordination

One instrument for co-ordinating activities in a shopping centre is the differential rents charged to the different tenants. Tenants usually pay a base rent plus a percentage rate based on sales. The charges differ among store types. In a detailed study commissioned by the Newfoundland Department of Municipal Affairs and Housing,[27] the following table of differential rents charged to different stores in Canadian regional shopping centres was reported. If those with lower rents also get preferred sites and exemptions from the common-area charges, the differential in rents may be even larger than those reported in table 23.[28]

Differential Rents and Market Power

It is sometimes alleged that rent differences reflect the lower bargaining power of independents as compared to the large chains and department stores when dealing with shopping centre owners. The policy problem is that there are also efficiency reasons why the differences exist. The independents do not have the same brand capital possessed by national chains or department stores. If a store from a chain brings in more customers because of its national advertising and reputation, the presence of the chain store is worth more to the independent than the presence of the independent is worth to the chain. In this case, the differential rents are a way of paying for the value rendered. Another factor is that the chains and department stores are worth more to the developer because financial institutions are more willing to provide mortgage financing if these firms are among the lessees, presumably because the chains and department stores are less likely to have financial difficulties and be unable to meet their lease requirements than the independents.

Table 23
Rent Levels—Canadian Regional Shopping Centres

Retail Outlet	Total Median Rent /Foot^2 ($)	Rate of Median Percentage Rent (%)
National Chain Department Store	2.62	2.0
Supermarket	3.05	1.5
Menswear	8.01	6.0
Books and Stationery	8.05	6.0
Ladies Specialty	9.06	6.0
Flowers	11.93	8.0
Men's and Boy's Shoes	13.00	6.0
Records and Tapes	14.46	6.0
Specialty Foods	19.52	7.5
Fast Food	20.60	7.0

Source: *Dollars and Cents of Shopping Centers*, 1978, Washington, D.C., Urban Land Institute, 1978 as cited in Deleuw Cather Canada Ltd., *Newfoundland Labrador Retail Development Study, 1982* (May 5, 1983).

Whether the differentials exceed the amounts justified on efficiency grounds is difficult to determine. Since the measurement problem in determining whether a rent schedule is inefficient and exploitive is considerable, the best social defence may be to ensure that there is sufficient competition among developers for sites. With competition, choosing an inefficient rent schedule puts a developer at a disadvantage.

Shopping Centre Locations and Local Planning: Differences between Public and Private Co-ordination

Cheaper land and the lower cost of putting together blocks of land of sufficient size made the shopping centre originally a suburban phenomenon. A developer is paid for putting together a shopping centre through the site rents and the increase in value of surrounding property he or she owns. However, after the downtown shopping areas suffered volume declines and bankruptcies as shoppers chose to frequent the new malls, a reaction occurred. City administrations became more helpful to developers with plans for assembling downtown shopping complexes, and planning restrictions increased in the suburbs.[29] As an illustration of how the increased concern with the impact of peripheral development on the core has manifested itself in Ottawa, the current city plan states:

A decade or so ago, there was a serious concern with respect to the diminishing retail dominance of downtown Ottawa. This concern led to the significant joint effort and contribution by various levels of government and the private sector to encourage the development of Rideau Centre.[30]

A modern regional shopping centre has a considerable impact on traffic, on the passenger flows for public transportation systems and on the fabric of life in a community. The co-ordination of these ancillary services with the features of the shopping centre is done politically through municipal and provincial bodies. These planning procedures take into account a number of considerations, including the effect on merchants in other areas of town.[31] In a period of growth, the shopping areas of a city are constantly being redefined, with competitive pressures from the new areas at the periphery and reconstruction responses from the core. In this ebb and flow, some centres become run-down and tacky and then are closed or refurbished.

The planning process both slows down change and directs it. Some moderation in the pace of change and in its nature may be economically efficient in that competition in the provision of selling space, under some circumstances, can lead to unnecessary duplication and premature development. There are many externalities generated by the retail business. One store may generate a flow of traffic that increases the sales of another, and the effects of both operating may be to increase congestion on roads for residents in the area.

To illustrate how a social loss may occur from making a mistake in timing, consider an area in which one regional shopping centre would make above-normal profits, but two would lose money. In this situation, contenders will try to pre-empt the market by building first. Competition would drive the opening date ahead until the losses from building early would balance the excess profits from having abrogated that right. In this case, the wealth of the community would be increased by making a deal with a single developer to delay construction and make an appropriate payment in order to receive an exclusive right. This arrangement would amount to selling in an auction the exclusive right to create a regional shopping centre in the area. Planning may simulate such an auction, with the payment from the developer being exacted through tax arrangements, through in-kind social investments such as placing a regional art gallery in the complex or, with corrupt local regimes, through bribes.

There are effects of a shopping centre on the rest of the community and vice versa which cannot be effectively co-ordinated commercially because of the costs of making the appropriate arrangements. Typically, this problem occurs because a large number of agents are involved and is resolved through political processes rather than private contracting. Political constraints are different from commercial ones, and the control exercised by a planning agency and a city council reflect this difference.[32] Sometimes change is slowed down, even when wealth in total would decrease as a result, because influential groups stand to lose from the change. Nevertheless, there is an incentive for the politicians to put together packages that combine the change with political "side payments" that transform the opposing group into supporters.

The current trend in Canada is that shopping centres are becoming larger and encompassing more service activities. The prognosis for the future is that shopping centres, co-ordinating traditional retailing and a number of services, will be integrated with office space and residential space in one complex. The organizational margin will be shifted, with a wider set of activities co-ordinated commercially rather than politically through planning and detailed zoning laws. The political control will be asserted over the general process rather than the detail.

NOTES

1. June 22, 1987.

2. A variant is the area development franchise, where a franchisee agrees to set up a minimum number of outlets in an area in a period.

3. Association of Canadian Franchisors (ACF), *Overview of Franchising in Canada* (Report prepared for DRIE undated), p. 18.

4. Payments are normally placed in a trust fund by the franchisor and then expended on brand name investments.

5. Substantial investments in the site which cannot be transferred to other uses may serve a similar purpose of creating a hostage that disciplines the franchisee. See Frank Mathewson, *The Role of Franchising in the Development of the Service Economy* (Fraser Institute working paper June 2, 1987) for a discussion of the role played by the up-front fee.

6. *Financial Post,* June 22, 1987.

7. Ibid.

8. An excellent discussion appears in Frank Mathewson, *The Role of Franchising in the Development of the Service Economy* (Fraser Institute working paper June 2, 1987). Other helpful sources are G.F. Mathewson and R. Winter, "The Economics of Franchise Contracts," *Journal of Law and Economics,* XXVIII (October 1985), and Paul H. Rubin, "The Theory of the Firm and the Structure of the Franchise Contract," *Journal of Law and Economics XXI* (1978).

9. June 22, 1987.

10. S. Luxenberg, *Roadside Empires: How the Chains Franchised America* (Viking Penguin 1985), p. 13.

11. A failure to write a restriction in the contract can cause a different outcome to occur under a franchise arrangement than would have with corporate control. One example concerns the Allentown franchisee of McDonald's Restaurants held by Harold Fulmer. Fulmer's franchise contract stipulated that his outlet must be open from 6:00 in the morning to 11:00 at night. In 1974, Fulmer started staying open 24 hours. McDonald's tried to stop him because they thought it would ruin their wholesome image, but the contract was permissive, and they realized they could not legally stop Fulmer. When the experiment was successful and the expected depreciation of the wholesome McDonald's image did not occur, McDonald's switched to supporting the concept.

S. Luxenberg, *Roadside Empires: How the Chains Franchised America* (Viking Penguin 1985), p. 58.

12. S. Luxenberg, *Roadside Empires: How the Chains Franchised America* (Viking Penguin 1985), p. 25.

13. K. M. Fong, "The New Competition Act and Franchising (Part I)," *Business & Law,* v. 3, no. 9 (September 1986), p. 66.

14. Association of Canadian Franchisors (ACF), *Overview of Franchising in Canada* (Report prepared for DRIE undated), p. 6.

15. According to the Association of Canadian Franchisors, a new franchisee with an established chain stood an 80 percent chance of succeeding, while a new independent store had only a 20 percent chance of succeeding.

16. *Financial Post,* June 22, 1987.

17. M.P. Kacker, *Transatlantic Trends in Retailing* (Quorum 1985), p. 104.

18. Laventhol & Horwath, *An Investigation of the International Expansion of Canadian Franchise Systems* (Spring 1987).

19. This phenomenon is well illustrated by the following account of imitation in the fast food business:

> After Wendy's opened, Judy's, Cindy's and Andy's began offering variations on the large-patty theme. The Wendy's concept consisted of thicker hamburgers served in restaurants featuring turn-of-the-century design motifs. Cindy's sought to bring higher-quality fast food to small towns in the southeast that had been overlooked by the national chains. Signs over Wendy's stores read "Wendy's Old-Fashioned Hamburgers" and displayed a picture of a girl with pigtails tied with ribbons. Cindy's sign said "Cindy's Ole Time Hamburgers" and featured a girl with pigtails tied with a ribbon. Luxenberg, *op cit.* p. 24.

20. City of Ottawa, *Official Plan: Commercial* (Issue paper undated), p. 6.

21. In 1973, the figure was 87 percent. See Statistics Canada, *Shopping Centres in Canada 1951–1973* (August 1976) for the definitions.

22. K mart annual report, p. 4.

23. Report of the Prince Edward Island Commission of Inquiry on Shopping Centres and Retail Stores, December 31, 1980, p. 152.

24. The alteration would often have to be accompanied by some side payments. That is of course what an ideal contract would achieve. Contracting requires owners of the rights to undertake the action to promise to change their behaviour and for this promise and the promises of payment to be enforceable. Sometimes there is no defined owner to contract with and sometimes enforcement is not economical. The continued existence of forgone gains from trade is only rational if some cost of co-ordination (of contracting) is preventing their achievement.

25. W. Stephenson, *The Store that Timothy Built* (McClelland and Stewart 1969), p. 159.

26. This monitoring function may provide another reason why some chains have both corporate-owned stores and franchises. The results from one can identify trouble areas in the other. During an earlier period, internal competition was encouraged within the Eaton's complex: "Eaton stores competed as fiercely with their own catalogue salesmen as they did with outsiders." Stephenson, p. 95.

27. Deleuw Cather Canada Ltd., *Newfoundland and Labrador Retail Development Study, 1982* (May 5, 1983), table 2-5. The *Annual Inventory of Shopping Centres* does not contain data on rentals by type of store.

28. In Deleuw Cather Canada Ltd., *Newfoundland and Labrador Retail Development Study, 1982* (May 5, 1983) it is asserted that the anchors often obtain these benefits (p. 2-17).

29. This is particularly true in Ontario, which initiated a Downtown Revitalization Program in 1976. Government loans were offered for downtown projects that met certain criteria and the Ontario Municipal Board created barriers to the development of peripheral malls.

30. Ibid., p. 6.

31. The official plan for the Regional Municipality of Ottawa-Carleton states that when considering the designation of a site for a regional shopping centre the following, among other things, should be considered: (a) the adequacy of the site for the purpose; (b) its proximity to transportation facilities, particularly freeways and rapid transit routes; (c) the impact of a regional shopping centre on surrounding land uses; (d) the impact of the proposed centre on the retail function of the central area and other shopping centres.

32. The contrasts in the two processes are highlighted by the difference between the co-ordinating done within the shopping centre by the owner and the co-ordinating of the impact of the shopping centre on the rest of the community that is accomplished through the planning process.

Chapter 8

CONCLUSION

The trade sector bridges production and consumption. Through its institutions information is processed about the demands of individuals and the costs of meeting them. Through its networks an item costing a few dollars can wend its way from a small town in Thailand to the tool box of the reluctant weekend handyman. Building and maintaining a fixed distribution system with this capability is an impressive accomplishment, but what is in place is more than that. A process exists with an inner dynamic. The stores of today are different from and better than those of yesterday; tomorrow's can be even better. This sector generates creative responses as well as systemic ones.

Distributors recognize and respond to the facts that their customers provide valuable inputs into shopping, that consumers are not well-informed about the values available, and that potential customers are suspicious that quality will be promised but not delivered. Whereas creative innovation in other sectors often takes a physical form, the better mousetrap phenomenon, the equivalent innovation in the distribution sector is a change in organizational form which better mobilizes the combined resources of the shopper and the shopkeeper.

This difference in the focus of innovation requires a different framework for analysis. Much can be learned from traditional statistical approaches to productivity in this sector, but much will be missed by them. Data on organizational evolution is published sporadically and, almost inevitably, it does not receive the same attention as more easily measured aggregates such as sales. Publication of an annual survey of organizational developments in the trade sector, of trends in private initiatives and in public responses, would improve understanding of this sector. Since governments have special rights to obtain data and need to gather much of the relevant data in the course of enforcing and modifying existing policy, a government-supported publication in this vein seems warranted.[1]

Some other specific suggestions can be derived from the discussions of various issues in this study. Among these are: (a) gathering more data on the inputs by shoppers, similar to those produced in the Canadian Time Use Pilot Study; (b) considering an exemption of the retail sector from comparable-worth initiatives; (c) examining carefully the case for extending many of the general legal obligations of employers towards full-time employees to part-time workers; (d) giving more publicity to misleading advertising convictions; (e) making retail price maintenance illegal only in cases where it supports cartel pricing; (f) extending the role of the private sector in the marketing of alcohol; and (g) maintaining as contestable as possible a process for the allocation of rights to develop large shopping centres.

Although suggestions can be drawn from the study, justifying specific policy reforms was not our objective. Instead, we have striven to present a perspective on the evolution of the sector and the roles of different players in that evolution that would be enlightening. In sector studies there appears to be an imperative for the analyst to come up with specific answers to the "problems" he or she identifies. We disagree with that approach. It is what voters and politicians consider to be problems and solutions that will be determinate. A policy analysis that suggests a framework for understanding and for guiding intervention is less dramatic but more constructive.

There is no question that government is an important player in the retail sector. It establishes and enforces laws on property, on fraud, on product liability, on labour market responsibilities, on combines, and on a host of other areas which are extremely important. It also gathers and disseminates information, and acts as a catalyst for private action. Sometimes it becomes a direct participant in the activity. We have discussed and documented the comparative advantage of the government in these different roles. Our overriding policy recommendation is that the government create an environment which is conducive to permitting creative organizational responses. To do that, the process of organizational evolution should be understood, and it is towards that important goal that this study is dedicated.